RAY McCAULEY: FAITH THAT FIGHTS FOR A NATION

Ray McCauley: Faith that Fights for a Nation

RON STEELE

STRUIK CHRISTIAN BOOKS

KINGSWAY PUBLICATIONS
EASTBOURNE

Unless otherwise indicated, biblical quotations are from the
New International Version © 1973, 1978, 1984 by the
International Bible Society.

Cover design by W. James Hammond

ISBNs
0 85476 315 5 (Kingsway)
1 86823 138 0 (Struik Christian Books)

Struik Christian Books Ltd
(A member of the Struik Publishing Group (Pty) Ltd)
Cornelis Struik House
80 McKenzie Street
Cape Town 8001
South Africa

Reg. No. 04/02203/06

Printed in Great Britain for
KINGSWAY PUBLICATIONS LTD
1 St Anne's Road, Eastbourne, E Sussex BN21 3UN by
Clays Ltd, St. Ives plc
Typeset by J&L Composition Ltd, Filey, North Yorkshire

Contents

PROLOGUE

A Preacher in Politics?

Since 1948 South Africa has been under a racist government system. This system, known worldwide as 'apartheid', which literally means to 'keep apart', has caused untold human damage in a nation where the minority White population has dominated the other races—Blacks, Indians and Coloureds (mixed race)—who make up the overwhelming majority.

Hardly a day has gone by in the past forty years without South Africa making the headlines in some newspaper or television transmission somewhere in the world because of her racist legislation. Throughout this time the White minority—presently about five million—has held total political sway over the other 30 million people of non-White races.

Besides the havoc it has caused in the social, educational and personal lives of millions, it has reaped international repercussions for South Africa, with harsh economic sanctions imposed and enforced by the United Nations.

The apartheid policy, of course, unfolded gradually. When the Afrikaner Nationalist Party came to power in 1948, the then Prime Minister Dr Danie Malan initiated the beginnings of vicious laws which would be placed on the statute books and render all non-Whites as second-class citizens. In fact, as the laws emerged and 'Grand Apartheid' became clearer under later Prime Ministers like J. G. Strydom and Dr Hendrick Verwoerd, Blacks were not even regarded as citizens of the country they had been born in.

As the nuts and bolts were tightened and apartheid legislation dominated every aspect of South African life, so the international community began to voice its disapproval. In the fifties few American or European leaders made any great protests. But in the sixties, when Dutch-born Prime Minister Dr Verwoerd (who survived one assassination attempt, but died later from an assassin's knife) led South Africa out of the Commonwealth, a new and protracted Cold War broke out.

It began with sports boycotts. South Africans, traditionally, are great sportsmen and women, having won international acclaim in the Olympic Games, on the rugby and cricket fields, in tennis, golf and boxing. With a few exceptions, most of the South African sports stars were, of course, Whites. Black sportsmen never got the same opportunity to train or to receive expert coaching, or to use first-class equipment and facilities. So the sports boycott was aimed specifically at Whites because they would be the ones to suffer.

South Africans found themselves barred from the 1964 Olympic Games in Tokyo. The boycott axe fell with a sickening thud on the MCC cricket tour when the then South African Prime Minister, John Vorster, refused to allow South African-born Basil D'Oliveira (a Coloured person) to be included in the touring side to South Africa.

Meanwhile the famous Springbok rugby teams laboured on, facing massive demonstrations in Britain in 1969 and continued harassment over the years, until they too were isolated from international matches.

South Africans have been banned from international football for decades now, and athletes and swimmers have suffered the same fate. Individual sports like golf, boxing and tennis have not been hit so hard by the boycotts, with many South Africans competing in these sports and winning.

Sports boycotts, of course, led to further restrictive measures. Few international entertainers have visited our shores in the past fifteen years.

On a larger scale South Africa faced an oil boycott, dwindling overseas investments, and an arms boycott. The final nail in the coffin came in the late eighties when overseas industrialists began pulling out of South Africa and heavier international sanctions were clamped on the country by the United Nations. Sanctions and disinvestment became buzzwords in the country. They brought Christians into the critical socio-political arena—and were the reason for another major division among the churches.

The church in South Africa has, of course, been a major factor in the whole apartheid saga. It is a fact that the Dutch Reformed Church helped to formulate the racist policies which were implemented by the Nationalist Government. The same quip that is applied to the British Conservative Party and the Church of England was applied to the Nationalist Party and the Dutch Reformed brethren—they were the National Party at prayer.

The architects of the heinous apartheid system cooled their consciences with a twisted and distorted interpretation of the Scriptures. The Nationalist Government proceeded unchecked on its way, tearing apart the human fabric of South Africa with the blessing of the church. The devil, it seemed, could take a holiday because he had found an ally among the saints he was supposed to be destroying!

But not all of the church supported apartheid. The Church of the Province (Anglican), the Methodists, Lutherans, Congregationalists, Presbyterians, Roman Catholics and others bravely took up the cause of the downtrodden Black majority. These churchmen were maligned as meddling in politics, or labelled communists by the Nationalist Government. With great courage and at great personal cost, these ministers (many of them White) refused to be bullied by the Nationalist Government and its all too efficient security police who were fiercely loyal to apartheid and believed all opponents of this ideology were seditious and a threat to the State.

Sitting on the sidelines, piously looking on, was another segment of the church—the evangelicals, Pentecostals and charismatics. Their doctrines of holiness had made them so 'otherworldly' that they became blinded to what the real issue of apartheid was all about. They believed that to oppose the National Party and its apartheid system meant 'stepping into politics'.

It hardly dawned on them that apartheid is not primarily a party-political issue, but rather a very basic matter of justice, mercy and righteousness. In other words a moral issue, which needed to be judged by Scripture.

Sadly, the happy-clappers and tongue-talkers missed the point and by default became party to the tragedy of apartheid. Even today some Pentecostal churches fail to recognise their guilt or their need to repent because of the role they played in not opposing apartheid. By refusing to get involved in opposing an unjust and wicked social system they, like the majority of Whites in the country, sat back and enjoyed the material fruits and wealth which accrued to them as a result of their exclusive place in society. Apartheid penalised the majority of the nation and reserved the best for a few Whites.

This pietistic, blinkered view on world affairs and everything secular, is the background of Ray McCauley as well. Yet, he has managed to shake off those shackles and finds himself on centre stage with the likes of a past Nobel Peace prize winner, Archbishop Desmond Tutu, Rev Frank Chikane, General Secretary of the South African Council of Churches, and former Moderator of the Dutch Reformed Church Professor Johan Heyns. This latter trio have, in different ways, been major players in the past few years in the struggle against apartheid.

In all fairness it must be said that the Dutch Reformed Church, especially under the bold and courageous leadership of Professor Heyns, eventually came to its senses and rejected apartheid as heresy. Not, of course, without some strong opposition from the ultra-conservative element within their denomination. But the Dutch Reformed Church's decision to abandon apartheid must be viewed as one of the major turning points in Afrikaner thinking in South Africa, influencing the political decisions of the ruling National Party which followed in ensuing years.

The decision by the Dutch Reformed Church had a ripple effect on other churches who previously adhered to racist policies, like the Pentecostal denomination. Some, sadly, are failing to move with the new spirit of reconciliation, while the two major Pentecostal denominations, the Apostolic Faith Mission and the Full Gospel Church of God, were very slow out of starting blocks and may suffer splits if the White leadership does not adapt swiftly to the changing climate.

Meanwhile the mainline Protestant and Roman Catholic churches have sat rather smugly on the sidelines, watching the metamorphosis of their racist brethren. In fact, they haven't been all that enthusiastic in welcoming back their erring brethren, showing a little apprehension at the evangelical zeal which is so characteristic of the Pentecostals.

But, all in all, it has been a sobering time in the history of the church in South Africa. Sobering as church leaders have had to admit their folly in doggedly following heretical racist theology, yet exciting as the church has, through the great political and social upheaval, been thrown together and is beginning to forge bonds of unity which will be needed as South Africa treads warily into an unknown political future.

So Ray McCauley has been caught up in these nation-shaking events. He has no great academic achievements. He holds no theological degrees. He does not come from a church background, and in ecclesiastical circles is regarded as coming 'from the wrong side of town'.

He is a flamboyant, charismatic pastor. He believes ardently in the reality of God in everyday life. He believes implicitly in divine healing. He speaks in tongues.

Yet his faith is not focused on heaven alone. He has stepped down from the security of his pulpit to involve himself in the daily life of a nation. He rubs shoulders with key political leaders and opinion-makers. He believes fiercely in God's destiny for his life, and in the part he believes he has been called to play in the shaping of a post-apartheid South Africa.

In 1979 Ray received a prophecy, which he believes is being fulfilled in his life and the nation of South Africa. It read, in part, '. . . I have raised you up for this hour and for this task . . . the world shall look to you and that nation [South Africa] as an example, when they shall see love flow from Black to White and from White to Black.'

Despite the fury of death and destruction which presently soil South Africa's struggle towards racial and political equality, Ray McCauley and others cling to their faith in God, and a belief that a radiant new day awaits South Africa.

I

The President Comes to Church

The lounge was spotless. The carpets freshly cleaned. The furniture precisely placed with every ornament and flower arrangement, making the room look like the front cover of a glossy magazine on interior decoration. However, there was one small item missing . . . an ashtray.

Now, since this was the pastoral lounge of the Rhema Church, cigarette smoking was, of course, taboo . . . until the State President came to church.

South Africa's recently-elected new President, F. W. de Klerk, giving a glimpse of his bold new leadership style which would irreversibly change the future of South Africa the following year, surprised staunch Afrikaner tradition by accepting an invitation to attend Rhema, a controversial charismatic church, in December 1989.

Rhema was founded in 1979 by ex-bodybuilding champion Ray McCauley. Despite much negative media reporting, it had reached a size and status that not even the Nationalist Government could ignore. Its 15,000-strong active membership made it by far the largest single church in the country. Even more significantly, though, in a nation tortured by bigotry and racism, Rhema's congregation was totally integrated and probably ranked as one of the largest multi-racial congregations in the world.

At first it was surprising to hear of Mr de Klerk's positive response to the Rhema invitation. It was extended with the knowledge that charismatic churches are not often regarded as of any real significance by politicians, and also that traditional Afrikaner religion looked down their noses at Christians who clapped and waved hands . . . and spoke in strange, so-called heavenly languages.

So it was against these odds that a telephone call suddenly galvanised the Rhema church into action to host the Head of State. In hindsight, of course, one realises that Mr de Klerk's decision to come to Rhema was something of a preview of the history-making decisions he would announce the following year, 1990, which would set the pace for a new, multi-racial, non-racialist South Africa. His presence in an integrated church service can now be seen as symbolic of something that was just around the corner.

Mr de Klerk was openly showing a new bold and courageous stand in breaking out of preconceived moulds—whether religious or political. His visit to Rhema was in his personal capacity; nevertheless, it entailed all the paraphernalia of security searches and the usual entourage of bodyguards who cling to their political charges.

Feverishly the Rhema leadership brushed up on its etiquette and protocol for the big day. Special parking was arranged, and seats carefully selected for Mr de

Klerk and his wife and, of course, the bodyguards. A gourmet cook, a student at Rhema's Bible school, was commissioned to prepare an elegant finger lunch, and a select few were chosen to join the special occasion after the service.

When the presidential vehicle drew up at the special parking bay everybody knew the drill, where they were to be and what they were to say. It seemed as though every conceivable item had been taken care of . . . until the President lit up a cigarette in the pastoral lounge.

I was present in the lounge when this 'calamity' struck. Ray and his wife Lyndie had welcomed Mr de Klerk and his wife Marietjie, and I had shut the door (with the bodyguards outside) as Ray offered the President a cup of tea.

Not trusting the none-too-domesticated Ray to do the tea honours, Lyndie and I decided to take charge. As I poured, I caught a movement out of the corner of my eye. The president had slipped out a gold-plated cigarette holder and was preparing to light up.

Crisis number one struck. I noticed the President hesitating as he put the cigarette to his lips. Was he having second thoughts about smoking in our lounge? No, he wasn't. It dawned on me that he was accustomed to someone flicking a light for him. And I had no lighter— nor were their any matches available.

Mr de Klerk, as we learnt later, is a heavy smoker, and after scratching around in his pockets produced a lighter and was soon puffing away. But now crisis number two had arisen: no ashtray. My despairing eyes now caught Lyndie's, who despite her loathing for cigarette smoke thought it unwise to rebuke a President.

I was almost prepared to let him dust the ash onto the floor or into his jacket pocket, but Lyndie seized a shallow jar normally reserved for a hoard of peppermints. It was empty. Lyndie thrust it into my hands and with a nonchalant gesture I produced an ashtray for Mr de Klerk's glowing cigarette.

After some small talk it was time to go through to the church auditorium. Ray, knowing how sensitive the political feelings of some of Rhema's Black members were (many are ANC sympathisers) wanted to avoid making too much fuss when Mr and Mrs de Klerk entered the church, and so we took them through a few minutes after the service had begun. This meant that the 5,500-strong congregation were standing, singing and clapping their hands to a lively Pentecostal song as I guided the presidential couple to their designated seats.

Ray and Lyndie, meanwhile, went onto the platform, and the service was soon in full swing. Although the charismatic praise-and-worship style was a new experience for the President, who came from a Dutch Reformed background, it was obvious he felt reasonably at ease. In fact, his relaxed and very personal approach gave his bodyguards a jolt when Lyndie, who was doing the announcements, asked newcomers to the church to stand up.

This is a normal occurrence in Rhema and VIPs are not expected to respond to this call. But Mr de Klerk turned to his wife, nudged her and in a loud whisper said: 'Come Marietjie, let's stand.' Almost caught napping, the two bodyguards sitting directly behind the presidential couple catapulted to their feet too.

The rest of the service continued as normal, with the de Klerks getting a warm ovation when introduced by Ray, who preached on 'The Beauty of our Heavenly City'. He preached in his normal forceful style, but for those who know him well, it was obvious that he was a bit nervous and concerned about not speaking for too long.

Afterwards, at the private buffet, chatting with Mr de Klerk for a while, Ray made a simple statement to the President, but with singular forcefulness. In charismatic cliché language one would have called it 'anointed'. As the President sat on the arm of one of the lounge chairs, cigarette in hand, Ray said: 'Sir, I just want to encourage you to do what is right in your heart. Many of your people will not understand and may even turn against you, but just do what you feel is right in your heart.'

At that time, December 1989, the ANC leader Nelson Mandela was still in jail on Robben Island. The ANC Party was banned and so, too, were all other activist Black political parties. Mr de Klerk, elected to office in September 1989, was a totally unknown quantity as a leader.

South Africa had just come out of the P. W. Botha era, a president who had ruled his cabinet colleagues with a dictatorial power, who had promised much to the country, but had failed dismally to bring about any meaningful change in the racist style of government. Now the relatively young F. W. de Klerk had assumed the leadership mantle of one of the most complex nations in the world, and 35 million people in South Africa were eagerly awaiting his first political decisions.

Here, in the pastoral lounge of Rhema, a minister of the gospel was giving the most simple words of encouragement, yet as events are unfolding in South Africa, it seems that President de Klerk is doing just that—following the dictates of his heart and not the sterile philosophy of political moguls.

In January 1990, Ray was part of a multi-church delegation which met for an hour with the President at the famous Union Buildings, in the capital city of Pretoria. Although not officially included in the delegation I managed to push my way in as an official church photographer. It was a delegation of eighteen people, and time was limited, so it was agreed to ask some specific questions, some political and others dealing with moral issues. Ray was not the spokesman for this group and it seemed unlikely that he would get an opportunity to say much in the discussion.

Yet, knowing Ray's bold character, I knew he would attempt to get a word in somewhere if he could. And so it was that, as the meeting was winding up, Ray grabbed an opportunity to say something. I was sitting at the far end of the massive oval table and strained to hear what he would say. It was an echo from the lounge at Rhema. 'Do what's right in your heart to do.'

I am not claiming, by any means, that Ray is the only person to have influenced the President. In fact, one of the most positive facets of the Nationalist Government, since the Dutch Reformed Church declared apartheid a heresy, has been their openness to receive godly counsel and to discover how many are committed Christians.

Many men, like Professor Johan Heyns and the Anglican Bishop Desmond Tutu, caught the ear and heart of the Government over the past years. Yet in some small way it seems that Ray's honest words of encouragement may have been a catalyst for some remarkable events in South Africa—words backed up by the millions of Christians around the world who have earnestly prayed for this pain-racked nation.

On February 2, 1990, President de Klerk made a momentous speech, one which totally altered the future course of South Africa and sounded the death knell to institutionalised apartheid.

In the full glare of the international media and with the nation's ears pricked for the occasion, Mr de Klerk announced the release of Nelson Mandela, after twenty-seven years in captivity. The ANC and all other Black so-called radical groups were unbanned, including the South African Communist Party—the latter causing an even bigger surprise than the release of Mandela, which had been mooted for months.

For over forty years the Nationalist Government had expressed a paranoic fear of Communism, branding almost anyone who displayed any liberal or Leftist leanings as Communist. President de Klerk, in a dramatic two-hour speech, unleashed a whole new energy force into the South African political spectrum by bringing Nelson Mandela onto the stage. Also unbanned was the avuncular Joe Slovo, then leader of the South African Communist Party. Both men were to figure prominently in Ray's life in the following months.

2

Mandela Row

Earlier, in 1989, Ray received news from what he regarded as an impeccable source, that the imprisoned Nelson Mandela had made a firm commitment to Christ as a result of watching a Billy Graham gospel telecast. It was exciting news, but it was to land Ray in a lot of hot water and drag him into a controversy that made media news at home and abroad.

Mr Mandela had become one of the most famous prisoners in the world. He received unprecedented international publicity, as he became a symbol of all that was wrong and oppressive in the South African apartheid system. Sent to jail in 1953 for committing acts of sabotage, Mr Mandela, a lawyer and up and coming leader in the ANC, had at his trial in Johannesburg indicated very strong Communist leanings, and since the ANC was exiled from South Africa it had come under greater Marxist domination. So when the news filtered out from Robben Island that Mandela was 'born again', it caused a major stir among many Christians.

The news of Mr Mandela's so-called born-again experience was first noted by Ray in a report in *The Star* newspaper in Johannesburg. They carried a story of an interview that appeared on BBC television between David Frost and Dr Billy Graham. In the interview Dr Graham mentioned that he had received a letter from Mr Mandela, in prison, in which he had indicated that he had watched a recent gospel crusade and had been moved to make a recommitment of his life to the Lord.

On the basis of this information Ray made some enquiries, and through a Christian who had access to the prison authorities ascertained that the newspaper report was correct. It was also confirmed that Mr Mandela, brought up as a member of the Methodist Church, regularly read his Bible and also received communion. Ray took the opportunity to write a personal letter to Mr Mandela, encouraging him in his Christian walk and assuring him of his prayers.

The news that Mr Mandela was a committed Christian quickly began to spread through the Pentecostal/evangelical camp, and got so distorted that some versions even had it that Ray had personally led Mr Mandela in the sinner's prayer! This underlined, again, just how naive White charismatic Christians can be, especially when it comes to political matters. The political climate in the country was such that it seemed inevitable that Mr Mandela would be released from prison and assume a powerful leadership role in South Africa.

White Christians, bombarded and almost brainwashed by Nationalist Government propaganda over the past forty years that the ANC and Mr Mandela were inherently evil, took brave new hope that Mr Mandela would suddenly emerge as a tongue-talking, hand-waving charismatic shouting 'Hallelujah' and 'Praise the Lord', and all the worries of the nation would be rolled away in a heavenly glory cloud.

Great, of course, was the disappointment of the Christians when the momentous day came in March 1990 when Mr Mandela was eventually released. There were scenes of great jubilation and high tension in Cape Town as the grey-haired, seventy-two-year-old made his first public speech in twenty-seven years. It was a speech riddled with anti-government and anti-apartheid clichés—without any reference to God or Christianity.

Of course, the release of Mr Mandela was the biggest international news of the week. Reporters worldwide clamoured for any story they could angle on Mr Mandela, and Ray got himself caught up in the Mandela media frenzy.

At the time of Mr Mandela's release, Ray and Rhema's Missions Director Gordon Calmeyer were in America. Ray was taking part in a major conference with evangelist James Robison in Dallas when the news came through. The fact that Ray was a reasonably prominent South African made him a target for the media and he was interviewed by several television stations, including some of the major networks.

Ray naturally expressed his delight at the ANC leader's release, especially in the light of his encounters with President de Klerk and his firm belief that the South African Government had turned its back on apartheid. In the interviews Ray made mention of Mr Mandela's Christianity and gave the account of his so-called prison conversion. It all made good copy for the journalists and the 'born again' claim began to circulate in the international media.

The story was picked up in London where Ray, passing through on his way back to South Africa, was interviewed by the Press and again told the 'Mandela is a Christian' story. Meanwhile, there was silence from Mr Mandela and the ANC, and for the time being the South African media avoided the Christianity issue, caught up rather in the euphoria of the man and the moment. Besides the release of Mr Mandela, the ANC and other Black political organisations were unbanned and there were a wealth of stories for the media to chase so that on the local front the Christianity of Mandela was not big news.

On returning to South Africa, Ray expressed some disappointment that Mr Mandela had indicated no Christian testimony in any of his public speeches, and decided to write again and encourage him to make known his Christian stand.

It is Ray's strong conviction that, despite the error of the Dutch Reformed Church, Christianity still offers the only hope for true reconciliation in South Africa, and that if prominent leaders would declare this it would provide the basis for a peaceful solution. However, as time went by, no response or even an acknowledgement of Ray's letters to Mr Mandela was received. During a visit to Britain in July of the same year, Ray was cornered again by the media about Mr Mandela's Christianity. Wary now of the situation Ray simply told reporters that they should rather ask Mr Mandela, personally, about his religious convictions.

Back in South Africa Mr Mandela's extolling of the PLO and other radical Arab leaders began to throw serious doubts on the issue. The White Christian community, needless to say, were more than disappointed, and despite all of Ray's efforts to make any contact with Mr Mandela the issue looked like fading away.

Not that Ray tried to sweep the issue under the carpet.

He got colleague Gordon Calmeyer to contact the Billy Graham organisation, who confirmed there had been correspondence with Mr Mandela, but it was private and preferred not to make it available for publication.

Just when it looked like the whole matter was over, it blew up again and this time made a national impact. It was sparked off by a public rally at the end of July 1990 to relaunch the South African Communist Party. The meeting was held on a Sunday in a sports stadium in Soweto, the sprawling Black suburb just west of Johannesburg. Almost 50,000 people turned out with the Hammer and Sickle flag emblazoning the main podium, and there seated underneath it were Mr Mandela and his wife Winnie, who was resplendent in red dress and red shoes for the occasion.

The main speaker at the event was SACP General Secretary Mr Joe Slovo, reputed to be a KGB colonel, and an avowed hard-line Marxist and self-confessed atheist. His speech took the normal 'power for the people' direction, but he also took the opportunity to quote from the Old Testament and then made the claim that if Jesus Christ had lived in South Africa he would have joined the ANC armed struggle to overthrow the government and liberate Blacks from apartheid. Slovo's line was typical of the 'liberation theology' developed and exploited so well in Latin America.

The next day 'Jesus would have joined the armed struggle' made the newspaper headlines, as well as pictures of Mr Mandela sitting placidly under the Red Flag. Ray had just returned from a church conference in Munich and after he'd caught up with the news decided that Slovo's remarks should not go unchallenged. If Mr Mandela was a Christian, how could he endorse the Communist Party by his presence at its launching?

I was given the task of preparing a Press statement and of calling a media conference. Ray also asked me to muster as much support as possible from other Christian leaders to join him in refuting Slovo and the Communist Party, which was the main purpose of the public challenge. The Mandela–Christianity matter was a side issue. But it became the main focus of the affair for the media.

Ray spent much of the night before the morning media conference speaking to church leaders to encourage them to back him in his stand against Slovo. Some of the most prominent leaders were contacted, including the Revd Dr Frank Chikane, the General Secretary of the South African Council of Churches, Bishop Manus Buthelezi, a prominent Lutheran leader, Professor Heyns, of the Dutch Reformed Church and several others. Bishop Tutu was out of the country at the time.

Sadly, the only positive response came from Professor Heyns and from Rev Chris Lodewyk, former Crusade Director for German evangelist Reinhard Bonnke, who returned from Frankfurt to establish a specialised ministry dedicated to reconciling the different race groups in South Africa. All the other leaders who were contacted either stalled for time or tried to persuade Ray to drop the matter because they thought it unwise to make any public challenge to Mr Mandela. Ray refused to back down, believing that a Christian stand was necessary. So the media conference went ahead.

The conference proved highly successful with several newspapers attending, including the *Weekly Mail*, regarded as being liberal Left, and the national TV, which flighted the event prominently in the evening news bulletins.

The thrust of Ray's media comments was to rebuff Mr Slovo and to challenge him and the Communist Party to state their attitude to the church in a post-apartheid South Africa. Further, he challenged Mr Mandela to publicly make his stand on Christianity and also asked the ANC, because of their apparent strong Marxist leanings, to make plain their policy on religious freedom.

Outside of the political arena, this challenge from Ray was the most serious confrontation the Liberation movement had so far faced, and it proved to be a most sensitive and vulnerable area for the ANC and, of course, for the Communist Party.

Although it was expected that there would be a backlash and a retort from Mr Slovo and the ANC, it came as a great surprise when a stinging reply, published the next day, came from Rev Frank Chikane, of the South African Council of Churches. It seemed that the usually verbose ANC had lost its voice. It was said that two prominent church leaders like Ray and Chikane were now seen to be slugging it out in the public media arena on an issue which many thought should have brought them together. However, such is the complexity of the South African political and church scene that nothing is ever predictable.

The SACC's statement ignored the blasphemous Slovo remarks and zeroed in on the challenge to Mr Mandela's Christianity and highlighted the perverted perceptions that South Africans have because of apartheid. Dr Chikane pointed out, quite correctly, in the SACC statement that the experience of Black Christians in South Africa is radically different from that of White Christians.

His statement added:

We (Blacks) have no experience of Communist oppression and attack on our faith. Our experience is that of oppression by Whites who claim to be Christians. Our experience is that of detention without trial and torture without any recourse to the course of justice by White people who claim to be Christians.

No Communist attacked us while we were worshipping and praying in our churches. It is apartheid forces in the name of defending Western Christian civilisation [meaning the apartheid system] who attacked us.

No Communist justified apartheid. It is Christians who developed an elaborate theological justification of an inhuman evil and of a racist apartheid system. Our experience, like that of Dr Mandela, is that it is White Communists who expressed solidarity with the oppressed Black majority first, while White Christians were supporting apartheid.

The call, therefore, for Mr Mandela to dissociate himself from the South African Communist Party or to declare his Christian commitment to all South Africans, by White Christians, is not only disturbing, but adds insult to injury. What we expect from White Christians, at this stage, is to confess their sins of brutal Black oppression over the past three and a half centuries, rather than preoccupy themselves with the 'rooi gevaar' [an Afrikaans term for the 'Red Danger' of Communism].

The Press statement went on to say that the ANC and the SA Communist Party both guaranteed freedom of religious expression.

There was, of course, no disputing the facts as laid out by the SACC statement that many so-called White Christians were responsible for apartheid, but it was distressing to see the blatant support for Communists who had cleverly exploited the racist problems of South Africa. It underlined a crafty disinformation message which has been disseminated among Black people, that Communism was not to be feared, even by Christians.

The South African Government shares the blame in helping to create this illusion, because at every

opportunity it blamed Communism for the racial clashes
in the country. The seeds of deception are now being
reaped.

Although Ray received wide support from Black and
White Christians and many non-Christians for his
challenge to Slovo and Mandela, it was obvious that
there was also disagreement, especially from many Black
Christians.

The media was clamouring for more copy on the
McCauley–Mandela clash, and after close consultation
with Ray I released a sharp rebuttal to the SACC
statement in which we accused Dr Chikane and the South
African Council of Churches of being 'racist'. We were
really in a war of words now. No other Pentecostal or
charismatic leaders attempted to join the debate.

I mention this because a few weeks later a letter from
one of the major Pentecostal denominations surfaced in
the columns of one of the daily newspapers, taking Ray
to task for claiming to be a leader of the Pentecostal
movement! No effort was made to defend the gospel,
but it displayed the petty jealousy of certain Pentecostal
leaders and, of course, why they are insignificant in
bringing any change in the socio-political order in the
country.

In Ray's public censure of the SACC he accused them
of trying to divide Christians into 'White' and 'Black'
camps by suggesting that Ray was speaking only for
White Christians.

Ray's statement added:

It saddens me that Dr Chikane has been swift to defend Mr
Mandela, yet he makes no attempt to defend the Christian
faith which was insulted publicly by Mr Joe Slovo (in Mr
Mandela's presence) . . . it is true, as Dr Chikane states, that
Black Christians have never suffered under Communism.
But I am warning that you cannot ignore a forty-year track

record of tyranny and persecution which happened to the Christians in Eastern Europe.

Ray emphasised that the challenge to Mr Mandela remained.

> If he cannot declare his Christianity then he stands the possibility of alienating over 70 per cent of the nation who call themselves Christians.
>
> I am not condoning the evils of apartheid, but I must warn South African Christians that we could get a form of political freedom and in the process lose our religious freedom and the soul of the nation.

At the same time Ray issued a challenge to a public debate on religious freedom with Joe Slovo, to which the Communist Party replied with a media statement saying it stood for 'complete freedom of religion and worship in a secular state'.

The SA Communist Party Press release also said:

> There are believers in our Party and some of them are still underground. We see no reason why a believer who accepts the policies and programme of our Party cannot join and actively participate in Party work.

It was certainly strange to read that Christians were members of a political party which espoused atheism and also strange that those they termed 'believers' were 'active' in the underground. To be 'active' in their terms is interpreted as being involved in clandestine military activity, usually of a directly violent nature.

In private we mocked and ridiculed the claim that the Communist party could conceivably have Christian members. Some months later we were forced to recant when a former avowed hardline Marxist believer, Behrendt Schuitema, made contact with us.

Schuitema, who had worked in the SA Communist

Party underground and had been a wanted man for many years in South Africa, had in recent times experienced a remarkable change of heart after accepting Jesus Christ as his personal Saviour.

Schuitema was so deeply touched by the love of Christ that he determined to remain within the Communist Party and even formed a Christian ministry called 'Comrades for Christ'. He continues to work actively in the East London area of Johannesburg and is a senior executive member of the Communist Party in his area and successfully winning people to Christ.

Before releasing his initial challenge to Slovo and Mandela, Ray had attempted to reach Bishop Desmond Tutu for his comments—and possible support. Bishop Tutu, a Nobel Peace prize recipient, and outspoken critic of the apartheid system, was away at the time, but he did send a letter to Ray. But instead of support it contained what is best described as a 'soft rebuke'.

In his letter to Ray Bishop Tutu made the telling point that when Black Christians were being castigated and condemned he (Ray) and other White Christian leaders had been silent.

Bishop Tutu then went on to say:

> I think Mr Mandela questions your right to question him when you did not, to our knowledge, question such glaringly unchristian conduct. For him you have no credibility to question him. And I agree.

The 'you weren't there when we needed you' chorus has become extremely common among Black leaders whenever a White, be he a church leader or not, makes a critical remark about situations pertaining to Blacks. There is a certain suspicion that such Whites are now trying to cover up for their wrongs of the past and are trying to win favour with Blacks for the future. Some truth may exist in that perception.

Yet the real truth, I believe, could be a reverse form of racism and a certain amount of arrogance, especially when it comes to the ANC and its supporters. It's an arrogance which many English-speaking Whites have had to put up with from Afrikaans-speaking Whites, especially the Government! All of which emphasises how prejudiced and intolerant the South African society has become because of apartheid. Division and mistrust are on every side, and it is these wounds that the church, somehow, must heal.

This is why Ray has recognised the need to introduce a strong social concern in Rhema and to go public on matters where Christian ethics and morality are being ridiculed or questioned. Having the largest multi-racial church in the country has given him a certain credibility to speak out, even if Mr Mandela and Bishop Tutu disagree.

Ray has recognised and acknowledged his short-comings of the past when it came to making a public stand against apartheid and the Government. However, some of the Black criticism of Ray's political position may have been unjustified, because few bothered to find out what the church has been doing in the practical area while some critics have spent much time on rhetorical crusades.

So who is Ray McCauley? Who is this church leader who speaks 'prophetically' to a State President? Who is this man who dares to challenge the revered ANC leader Nelson Mandela? What is his pedigree? And how has he become a major spiritual influence in the cataclysmic socio-political upheaval in South Africa?

3
From Schoolboy to Bouncer

Ray's early school days were at the Norwood Primary School, in Johannesburg. He was the third born of four sons, on October 1, 1949. His school career revolved almost solely around sport. Academic achievements were sidelined. In fact, it was only sheer kindness which got him through his first year at school.

He showed little inclination to apply himself to learning, being far more interested in kicking a football or throwing a cricket ball. A significant remark appeared on the bottom of his first report card he received in 1955: 'Raynor is a very good story-teller.' A hidden talent that would one day be fully exploited from pulpits around the world. But for little Ray, sport was king. And his father, Jimmy, gave him and the rest of his sons every encouragement.

His father had been a keen sportsman, playing first team football for the East Rand club of Boksburg. He might have gone further with his football career if it had not been interrupted by the Second World War. His father's sporting interests also extended to horseracing and he made his living as a professional gambler. He was also an avid card player, thinking nothing of engaging in marathon two-day long card games.

Ray's father became a bookmaker and a respected member of the gambling fraternity of Johannesburg. When it seemed that Lady Luck had deserted him, and times got hard, he would take a job selling second-hand cars.

Ray's young days were spent in the middle-class Johannesburg suburb of Norwood, where the McCauleys owned a modest little house at 57 Algin Road. The whole neighbourhood came to know the McCauley clan as the boys—Jimmy, George, Ray and baby Alan—grew up. In fact, when he was eight years old, young Ray was the gossip of the neighbourhood when he was caught smoking at school. The headmaster paraded the young boy before the whole school at the morning assembly. But Ray took it all in his stride. It was youthful experimentation and adventure. Smoking, in fact, never appealed to him at all.

The incident was soon forgotten, but the neighbours sometimes despaired at the goings on at 57 Algin Road. The boys were wild and enthusiastic, always full of mischief. They even played soccer in the lounge, smashing ornaments. If they weren't fighting the neighbours' kids, they were fighting one another.

When Ray was about ten years old, his mother Doreen, a quiet woman by nature and worried by the insecurity of the gambling profession of her husband, began to drink heavily. Although it obviously caused some disharmony between husband and wife, it made no visible impact on Ray's outlook on life. He simply saw his mother's drinking as just another household problem.

He loved her very much and never allowed it to gnaw away at his emotions. Instead he lost himself in the hurly-burly of sport.

On the sporting field Ray soon got into the school soccer and cricket team, as well as boxing as a junior in the under-40lbs weight division. For his age Ray was on the small size, but what he lacked in stature and build he made up with fierce determination and courage. He still shines a few of the miniature trophies he won from those days in the square ring.

Elder brother Jimmy was also a keen sportsman and in fact played for the South African Schools XI in the Sixties. When Ray reached high school (Highlands North), he joined the famous South African soccer club, Balfour Park, and was in the under-14 team which won league and cup titles.

They were thrilling days for young Ray. He would rush home from school to change into his football togs and dash off to the Balfour Park sportsfields at 3 o'clock in the afternoon to practise, often not getting home until 8 o'clock in the evening.

One of the biggest delights of those young football days was when the juniors would have dinner with the senior club players, among whom was Ray's boyhood hero, Springbok soccer star Basil Hauser. It was this famous football personality who got Ray interested in weight-training, something which was to become an overriding passion when he left school.

Despite the tremendous amount of energy expended on the cricket and football fields, Ray tended to be on the stocky side and his football hero advised him to start weight-training to turn the surplus fat into muscle.

At about this time the McCauley family were forced to sell their Norwood house (gambling debts were mounting) and move to the Johannesburg flatland suburb of Hillbrow where they lived in Laverne Court, in Paul Nel Street.

Ray continued to attend Highlands North School and by now was in standard eight. When the end of the year reports arrived, Ray shamefully handed his dad a report card which showed that he had failed. Ray took it badly, knowing that he had let his father down, who insisted that Ray stay for another year and rewrite his standard eight. He was not the only boy who had failed, and with his tatty academic reputation Ray found himself in a class of 'no-hopers'.

A curious thing happened one day when Ray was suddenly called to the headmaster's study. Ray was baffled and wondered what crime he had committed this time! He was amazed when his headmaster did not reprimand him for any misdemeanour, but merely gave him a lecture on the value of academic achievement. 'You have the potential to do your matric examinations,' encouraged the headmaster.

But books and studying were not part of Ray's life. He wanted to achieve success, and sport looked the likely avenue by which he could gain this goal. He rejected the encouragement and did just enough to get through standard eight and obtain a school-leaver's certificate.

In December 1964 Ray walked through the gates at Highlands North High School for the last time. Now he was going out into the world and he was going to let it know who Ray McCauley really was. The chase for success and fame was on.

Armed with his school-leaver's certificate he set out to find a job. He was sixteen and had only one ambition—to become somebody that people would admire and look up to. His choice, for a young teenager who was heavily into physical fitness and bodybuilding, caused a few raised eyebrows. He became an apprentice hairdresser, specialising in hair tinting!

This strange choice did not last long. He soon realised his desire for a macho image was not enhanced by working in the effeminate atmosphere of a hair salon. He now began to spend more time doing weight-training and it struck him that this was the way to achieve not only success, but also respect.

While working out at a Hillbrow health studio he met famous bodybuilding stars like Dougie Baggott, who won the Mr South Africa title in 1964, and the legendary Reg Park, a Mr Universe champion.

It was the rugged Doug Baggot who won the attention of the teenage McCauley. He made the older muscleman his idol. Baggott was not only one of the country's best bodybuilders, but succeeded in winning international titles in judo. Young Ray started off as a 'hanger on', following Baggott into bars and clubs to get a glimpse of his hero dealing with trouble-makers. Soon Ray was working with Baggott as a bouncer in night clubs and discotheques.

As a result he became more involved in the night life of Johannesburg, and when his middle brother, George, opened up the Go-Go Club in Hillbrow, Ray was offered a job. He stood at the door each night, collecting entrance money and, despite his youth, his impressive muscular stature ensured that nobody tried to get in without paying. This started him off on the club beat. It suited his lifestyle to a tee.

During weekdays the clubs would usually close their doors at about midnight and Ray would then go home (he still lived with his parents) and would not rise until about 10 o'clock in the morning. He would then take three or four hours working out in the gymnasium, spending the afternoon in a cinema before going to work at about 8 o'clock in the evening.

At weekends the pattern changed slightly, because the clubs usually closed much later and then Ray and his friends would head for another nightclub, living it up until the sun was rising over the city.

During this five-year period Ray worked at some of the most famous Johannesburg night spots. Amazingly, he gained no scars during all this time. In fact, he never even suffered the indignity of a black eye. His secret was a very simple one. He never drank alcohol, and so was always sober and more than capable of handling any rough-house situation when it erupted at any of the clubs. He also learnt from Dougie Baggott never to go looking for a fight. The impressive duo of solid muscle landed in several brawls over the years, but Ray always managed to look after his clean-cut features and flashing Hollywood smile, while Baggott was not so fortunate. He once had a piece bitten off his ear, and on another occasion was stabbed.

Ray's strenuous training and extraordinary diet put considerable strain on the household budget. As a youngster he had been a normal eater. Now, as a dedicated bodybuilder, his appetite had become gigantic.

His father recalls, with a rueful smile, the occasion when American muscleman Frank Zane stayed at the McCauley residence and they decided to go on a meat and water diet. Mr McCauley had to hire a special domestic servant just to cook for them. They were eating four times a day and each sitting consisted of huge steaks. His father became so embarrassed about the amount of meat he was buying from the one butcher that, in order to save face, he rotated his purchases among three butchers.

Ray was enjoying his life. At twenty years of age he had the physique of a Greek god. His 'job' as a nightclub bouncer gave him opportunity to show off his strength and to ensure a steady flow of female admirers.

And yet, looking back at those days, he admits now that sometimes, when away from the clanking sound and sweat of the gym and the blaring music and flashing lights of the discos, he found himself pondering whether his popularity really could satisfy the deeper yearning that fretted deep inside him. There was, he recalls, an emptiness in his life, and he wondered at the time how he could find true fulfilment. Despite his lack of academic qualifications he was no fool. He was learning quickly in the school of life.

His religious experience had been almost non-existent. As a child he hardly ever went to Sunday school. There had been a brief interlude with church when he was about ten years old. One day, while playing on the street outside the family home, a battered old car came spluttering down the road, and out stepped a young minister, who was pioneering a Pentecostal church in the neighbourhood. His name was Doug Fisher and, unknown to him, the young kid in short trousers, kicking a ball on the pavement, would one day stand at the altar of the church he would establish in the area. But that was not to be for another ten years.

Fisher, who came from the southern suburbs of Johannesburg—a poorer area— spoke to the McCauley boys, who were playing in the street. Fisher, who knew the language of the streets, told them how he had once been a 'joller' and the boys listened. They had never heard a minister of religion use the slang of the street gangs, and his ability to communicate by means of ordinary language probably made some impression on the youngsters.

Certainly some spark was ignited, because Ray remembers that he went to the church that Fisher had started in a house and then his brother George took him to a nearby Methodist church on a few occasions. Outside of that brief encounter young Ray had little contact with the gospel.

Despite the lack of any serious religious convictions the McCauley household was not entirely godless. Ray's mother came from a religious family and he remembers that she sometimes prayed. His grandmother (on his father's side) was a staunch Roman Catholic who was an incorrigible gambler. She sometimes brushed with the law, so her religious beliefs didn't make much impact on the family.

The flirtation with church soon faded and Ray went on his way. In the meanwhile Fisher's tiny church grew and in the course of time acquired an associate pastor. At that moment Carl Cronje entered the scene. He was a young, dynamic Christian with not only a burning zeal, but an intellect that commanded the respect of his peers and gained him favour in influential circles.

Young Cronje, fired by the bestselling book *The Cross and the Switchblade* by American evangelist David Wilkerson, began a Teen Challenge Mission in the bustling flatland of Hillbrow. This concrete jungle of apartments sits on the northern brow of a hill over-looking South Africa's busiest city, Johannesburg. It has always boasted a cosmopolitan population, with a constant changing and moving community, and is a haven for runaway teenagers, drug addicts and alcoholics. At night, when the seamy side of life appeared, it was here that Carl Cronje busied himself working among teenagers who had run away from home, or who were on the drug trail.

During the week Carl dropped into a gymnasium in the suburb of Orange Grove where Ray worked out, and the two men first met. It was a meeting that was destined to have a tremendous influence not only on Ray's life, but on the lives of countless thousands of people in South Africa and overseas.

At the time neither men knew the divine plan that had brought them together in the busy gym. Ray and Carl began swopping conversation and a friendship grew. When Ray discovered that Carl was a preacher, he was highly impressed. Unlike the stereotype sombre-clad, dog-collared priest, Cronje was very much 'one of the boys', ready to swop a joke. After a while Carl approached Ray to help him in his Teen Challenge mission in Hillbrow. He figured that Ray's lifestyle was free of drugs and alcohol and that his clean-living image would be a fine example to the dozens of derelict youngsters with whom he was working.

That invitation was followed by another: would Ray come to church? Carl, who now lives and works in Durban, fondly recalls his first meeting with Ray and the events which led to his accepting an invitation to come to church.

'I was working out in the gym, sweating and heaving, when Ray came in. He had just returned from an overseas trip and he looked huge and superbly fit.

'His hair was shoulder length. We introduced ourselves and he was fascinated when he heard I was a preacher. I was immediately struck by his sincerity. In fact, this is a hallmark of Ray—his sincerity.

'Later, I invited him to church, I think maybe because I wanted to prove to him that I really was a preacher. So, one Sunday evening, I took Ray to the church where I was a pastor. That night, to my great disappointment, he did not respond to the altar call. But he came again and I must confess that this was the first and only time that I ever prepared a sermon specifically for a person. I felt no compunction about it. I deliberately prepared the sermon for Ray, believing that he would accept Jesus.

'I preached on Adam and Eve and of their vain attempt to hide their nakedness from God, making the application that it was useless for us to try and hide behind anything, and that we may as well be honest and accept God's salvation. When I gave the appeal, my eyes fixed on where Ray was sitting and I was not surprised when his hand shot up.'

Although Ray made a firm decision and accepted Jesus Christ, Carl admits that there were times when he despaired at the lack of any outward spiritual growth— even after several years. Yet despite Ray's apparent lack of Christian growth, he never refused to be counted for Christ no matter who was in the church.

He came to church sporadically, bringing with him many of his friends, and when called upon to give a testimony would never hesitate to do so.

Ray's conversion to Christ came when he was twenty years old. He was enjoying fame and popularity as a bodybuilder, having only recently won the Junior Mr Republic title. Inwardly, he knew he had a spiritual experience and that Jesus Christ was no longer just an historical character or a name that was blasphemed and used when you felt like cursing. However, he admits to feeling no special 'call' on his life, except to share his testimony when an opportunity arose.

For the next nine years he travelled around South Africa and occasionally overseas, talking to young people and urging them to commit their lives to the Lord. Soon after becoming a Christian, Ray met a young Welshman, Brian Gibson, a former pop singer from Britain. Gibson came to South Africa in 1968 and settled in Durban. Here he established a thriving antique business and became a notable success as a folk singer at a popular nightclub in Durban. He gave much of this up when he gave his heart to Jesus.

Soon after meeting, the two young men began travelling together, visiting schools and universities. Brian would sing and Ray would give a rippling muscle exhibition. Then they'd both give their testimonies. They made a formidable and unusual duo, and hundreds of young people committed their lives to Christ.

On one occasion Ray and Brian decided to preach the gospel at a mine compound at Crown Mines, on the southern outskirts of Johannesburg. It was a night meeting and the pair drove out in Ray's car and parked in a field near the dowdy and weathered red-brick, single-storey dormitories which housed several hundred Black mine workers. The only lighting they had was from the car headlights. It was the first time they had used a megaphone.

It proved a comical evening at the start with Brian trying to play the guitar and use a megaphone at the same time. The small group of miners gathered around, but were not impressed, and some nasty remarks were voiced. Things were beginning to look quite serious, and the two feared at one stage that the mob might turn on them. It was at this moment that Brian called out to the hostile crowd that God loved the Black man as much as he loved the White man, and that God would demonstrate his power in their midst. He told them to bring one of their friends forward who was sick. Ray remembers today that when he heard Brian's challenge he froze, thinking of the negative consequences of what sounded like an audacious statement. Brian, though, boldly carried on, urging the people to bring out a sick person.

The miners responded by carrying out a colleague of theirs who worked in the local pay office. He was a cripple and known to all the miners. They were determined to put Brian's statement to the test. Ray admits that he hardly closed his eyes as Brian prayed for the sick man. But to his—and everyone's—amazement the crippled man began to walk and dance. And so did Ray. It was one of many great experiences the two have shared in a life-long Christian friendship.

As the years passed Ray felt a desire to work among the poor. This led him to become involved in the old and crumbling suburb of Doornfontein, which surrounds the world famous Ellis Park sports stadium on the east side of Johannesburg. It was here that Ray saw the agonising consequences of prostitution, alcoholism, drug taking, child abuse and poverty. He obtained permission to use a recreational hall in the area, and each weekend would arrive at the hall loaded with food and clothing for the children. He also faithfully told them the gospel.

Sometimes, while preaching, he could hardly see to the far wall because of the haze of smoke from dozens of young people smoking marijuana. Those experiences, learnt among the poor and destitute, have kept him in good stead to this day.

4
Year of Decision

The year 1974 was a momentous one for Ray McCauley. When the sirens and motor car hooters had heralded the New Year, Ray's thoughts turned to the Mr Universe championships which were being staged in London that year.

Now that the festive season was over, with its excessive eating, Ray determined to concentrate on his dream of international sporting success. He spent hours every day sculpturing his muscles for the big London event. In May 1974 Ray, with every fibre of his being directed at perfecting his body, knew he had an outstanding chance of doing well at the international event in London. Then 24 years old, he had already made a name for himself, winning the Junior Mr South Africa title and then, a year later, the Mr Republic title. He had turned professional and recently finished runner-up in the Mr South Africa contest.

For every bodybuilder the Mr Universe competition

is the goal for which they all strive, and Ray still remembers arriving in London and seeing for the first time some of the great bodybuilders of the world.

'There I was, with all these famous bodybuilders, faces that you normally only saw in the magazines. It was a thrill to just work out and train in the gym with them.'

He still vividly recalls the day of the competition. 'I awoke and had a look at myself in the mirror, and began to cry. I couldn't believe how I'd hit my peak at the right time, and the condition of my body was better than I ever thought it could be. I knew then that I could cause a few upsets in this competition. I'd always battled with my weight. In fact, I'd have to diet for up to nine months of a year to be able to stay in peak condition.'

On that day Ray was, indeed, the classic picture of the young Adonis. At 1·78m (5ft 10ins) he weighed a perfect 84kg (185lbs, 13st 3lb). His muscles rolled and bulged in a harmony of glistening flesh. All the dieting and weight training had paid off.

That afternoon Ray walked out onto the stage in front of an audience of several thousand people. He did his individual poses and then returned with the group to complete another session of posing for the judges. When the announcement came that he had been placed third, Ray recalls that his emotions were those of supreme elation.

But after his triumphant return home the glamour soon wore off. He was still determined to be a witness for the Lord, and believed that God had given him this success to open more doors to do exhibitions and to give his testimony. Yet he became more and more aware that there was a deeper meaning to his life.

He decided that God must come first and that some of his former ways would have to change. The man who had spent most of his life 'pumping iron', had finally found his first love—Jesus Christ. The success and glamour of sporting achievements gave only fleeting satisfaction, and he realised now that his previous commitment to God had been too shallow. Looking back now he realises that he had reached a major crossroad: his will, or God's? His decision was to submit his own will and take the first faltering steps along a Royal and Holy Highway that would lead him into a worldwide ministry for Jesus Christ.

Some while after this momentous decision Ray had been visiting at a friend's house and had been witnessing to some people. Among those there was a young girl, Lyndie Trehair.

Ray had met her previously and invited her out, but she had turned him down. Later she heard the gospel and accepted the Lord, and the next time Ray invited her out she accepted.

Romance blossomed and they were engaged in August 1975 and another piece in the puzzle of Ray's destiny fell into place.

Ray and Lyndie were married at St Luke's church, in the Johannesburg suburb of Orchards, on 13th March 1976. During their engagement there had been a deep commitment to each other. Previously Ray had been involved with other women, but when he met Lyndie, the wandering eye was dulled.

After she had given her life to Jesus, Lyndie quickly severed relations with other boyfriends. Ray in fact became almost Victorian in his attitude, refusing even to kiss Lyndie in the six months before their marriage!

Although Ray was being drawn into a deeper spiritual life, both were poorly prepared for the rigours of a marriage partnership. Reflecting back on those early days Lyndie admits that they started arguing from the first waltz, which was danced to the popular hit of the time, 'The Last Waltz'!

Life for the young couple was filled with seemingly endless rows and disagreements. Their mutual love for the things of God managed to keep a very tempestuous marriage on course, but the strain and tension were often unbearable for Lyndie. Some of the tension was caused by the fact that they came from very different cultural backgrounds. Lyndie came from a conservative, organised, British-style background. In contrast, Ray's upbringing had been influenced by Lebanese culture, expressed mainly through his beloved grandmother.

In practical terms this meant that Ray was used to an open house policy. At his parents' home any number of guests (family or friends) could arrive for meals at any hour, as there was always a full-time cook on hand. It was only natural, Ray felt, that the same happy attitude towards hospitality should exist when he and Lyndie set up their own home. The difficulty was that Lyndie, with more conservative upbringing, could not handle the unorganised lifestyle and behaviour of Ray's friends.

By now Ray had opened up two health studios and become a reasonably successful businessman, but still very much 'one of the boys'. It was nothing for him to arrive home with four or five friends at ten o'clock at night and expect Lyndie to prepare a massive dinner of roast chicken, leg of lamb and roast beef, only to find that she had prepared an intimate dinner for two. It was small wonder that incidents like this set her off in a fuming rage.

Then there were close friends like Brian Gibson who, when in Johannesburg, would turn up at the McCauley home at one o'clock in the morning looking for a place to sleep. Brian, a longtime friend who nowadays gives advance warning, would simply waltz through to the lounge, lie down on the carpet and go to sleep. When Lyndie came through the next morning to check on her unexpected guest, he would be gone! As the privacy of her home was continually invaded, Lyndie could be forgiven for thinking she had joined a boy scout group.

On several occasions frustration drove her to threaten to leave home and return to her parents. In fact Ray remembers Lyndie packing her bags and telling him it was all over. When this happened Ray would insist that Lyndie take her baleful-looking bassett hound Clementine with her. . . .

Lyndie, clutching suitcases and handbag would tug and pull at Clementine's lead, but the droopy-eared hound refused to budge. The scene would produce such comedy that Lyndie and Ray would end up in each other's arms, laughing at the absurdity of the situation.

Shortly after their marriage Ray had the opportunity of doing a tour of America and Ireland with the Revd Tony Louch and the Revd Keith Strugnell, who ran an organisation called Go-Tell, involved in Christian films and entertainment. They were in fact responsible for bringing out Cliff Richard to South Africa on several occasions. These two men had become good friends of Ray, and it had been at Tony's church where Ray's granny and parents had made decisions to accept the Lord as their personal Saviour.

Ray went to America where he gave his testimony to youth groups and in churches. They also arranged for Ray to appear on some major American Christian television stations like the PTL Club and the 700 Club, hosted by Pat Robertson, founder of the Christian Broadcasting Network.

While in South Africa Ray and Lyndie were given some books and audio cassettes of Kenneth E. Hagin. The articles in the magazine gripped Ray's attention, and something inside him made him long to know more about the teaching and messages he read and listened to. So when Tony Louch and Keith Strugnell organised the tour to America, Ray determined to make a special trip to Tulsa to see Kenneth Hagin Jnr to find out whether he could go to Bible school there.

Ray made the excursion to Tulsa, but never had an opportunity to discuss anything with Mr Hagin. Ray arrived at the Rhema offices in Tulsa without an appointment, to discover that Hagin Jnr was on his way to the airport. They exchanged brief greetings in a corridor before the American rushed off to catch his plane.

Ray was bitterly disappointed and Keith Strugnell, who was sharing a room with him in a Tulsa hotel at the time, recalls how depressed he was at the time. It was while Keith was trying to console Ray that Tony Louch telephoned from another city in America, and when he heard how badly Ray had taken the missed meeting, offered to pay for Ray's tuition—if he could later on gain a place in the Rhema Bible Training Centre.

On his return to South Africa Ray continued working in his health studios, but his experiences in America and the longing in his heart steered his thoughts towards preparing for the ministry. However, the bumpy marriage relationship was a mutual concern.

When the couple look back today they fully acknowledge that it was only the grace of God that held them together in the first eighteen months, and with Ray talking about his desire to become a minister of religion, there was an added dimension to their problem.

Ray's desire was not shared by Lyndie, although she did not in any way try to stop him from responding to the divine call. Adding to the confusion at that time was the advice of a well-meaning acquaintance who told Ray that the best thing to do was divorce Lyndie as she would never be any good in the ministry! Lyndie, although she never envisaged herself involved in ministry, encouraged Ray to get the best possible Bible school training if he intended to become a full-time minister of the gospel.

This uncertainty and confusion about their future led to further arguments. Ray was determined to go overseas to study, even if Lyndie did not want to join him. Some of the 'advice' they received from Christian friends at that time added to the muddle they found themselves in.

Lyndie recalls: 'If we had received wise marriage counsel and had the knowledge of God's word which we have now, we would never have gone through such a difficult time.

'One night, after having discussed divorce, and who would take what from our assets, we went to bed. I began to doze off, then suddenly sat up in bed and said to Ray, "We can't get divorced—we can't disappoint Jesus."' And on that decision the foundation for a new life together was built. The decision, it seems, initiated a series of divine appointments. A holy hour had struck in heaven. The time to bring Ray and Lyndie into a new spiritual dimension had arrived.

The future spin-off, of course, when Ray and Lyndie did enter the full-time ministry, was to make them well able to encourage married couples to stick together, no matter how serious the troubles, faults and failures may be. Trusting God's word and obeying it brought them through a marriage that looked like ending in a divorce court.

In the meantime a minister friend, Robert Forsyth, who was an associate minister with Tony Louch, invited Kenneth Hagin Jnr to visit South Africa, and Ray was asked to look after the American and chauffeur him while he was in Johannesburg. Ray was amazed at how God was bringing to pass the desire of his heart to meet Kenneth Hagin Jnr—not in an office, but actually to be at his side for three whole weeks. The disillusionment of the past year was replaced by a sense of keen anticipation. Although Ray was still a novice in those days when it came to understanding the leading of God's Spirit, he knew that God was doing something and that he was in the centre of it.

Not only did Ray drive Kenneth Hagin around, but also had him staying at his home. It was in this environment that Ray and Lyndie recognised that this man of God was somehow different. Lyndie, who had brazenly puffed at her cigarettes in front of other ministers of the gospel, was now conscience-stricken and could not bring herself to light up. The couple were deeply impressed by the American's manner of speech and his impeccable lifestyle, which was in direct contrast to some of their experiences with other Christians and ministers whom they had previously known and respected.

Ray and Lyndie went to several meetings with Kenneth Hagin Jnr, and it was in the Central Methodist Church in Johannesburg in January 1977 that Ray first witnessed the power of God when people fell on the floor as if they had fainted. Later he was to identify this with the charismatic term of being 'slain in the Spirit'.

They watched in holy awe as Hagin prayed for the sick and people began to respond with testimonies of their healing. These meetings, and personal conversations with Hagin Jnr, made the couple realise how shallow their previous Christian experience had been. They acknowledged that one could not tolerate sin and expect to live a godly life. They saw in Hagin a man who not only preached with power and authority, but also lived a dedicated life.

Ray poured out his yearning to Hagin to go to Tulsa and study at Rhema. Mr Hagin, who had quietly watched and observed the McCauleys and also prayed about them, provided the answer. On the day he was scheduled to leave South Africa, Ray and Lyndie drove Hagin to Jan Smuts international airport. Mr Hagin was sitting in the front with Ray when he suddenly turned round and fixed his dark, brown eyes on Lyndie and bluntly asked her: 'Will you come to Bible school if we give you a bursary? I don't want you to go home and think about it. I must have your decision now. Is it "yes" or "no"? You must give the answer now.'

Ray recalls how his knuckles whitened as he tightened his grip on the steering wheel. Lyndie's green eyes evaded the penetrating stare of Hagin's eyes, but then she looked up and said: 'Yes.'

5

The Word of Faith

Ray and Lyndie arrived in Tulsa to attend the Rhema Bible Training Centre in July 1978. They were in time for the annual Camp Meeting hosted by Kenneth Hagin Ministries. Once Camp Meeting had finished, Ray and Lyndie found themselves alone in Tulsa, waiting until the Bible school reopened in September. The few friends and acquaintances that they knew were all away on holiday. The McCauleys felt dreadfully isolated in a strange and new city.

Mark Brazee, who had visited South Africa with Kenneth Hagin Jnr the previous year, willingly showed the McCauleys around Tulsa during the Camp Meeting week, and helped them find an apartment which was to be their home for the next ten months. Money was short: the young couple had $400 with which to buy a car.

It was at this time that Ray contacted an old friend from the international musical group 'Living Sound'. Terry Law, director of the group, told them he had a motor car for sale. It had belonged to his mother. It was a 1968 V-8 Oldsmobile. It had no airconditioning, which made driving in Tulsa in mid-summer almost unbearable as temperatures soared as high as 43°C (110°F) in the shade. Ray would often drive around in a bathing costume, with all the windows wide open, trying to keep cool. He still arrived dripping wet from perspiration. He lost several inches around his waist during his stay in Tulsa.

Their way of life was completely altered, including their eating habits. Instead of thick, juicy steaks Ray discovered that his staple diet for the next ten months consisted mainly of wholewheat bread, sweetcorn, and canned Campbell's soups.

The shock of being separated from her parents, away from the security of her own home, sent Lyndie into a steep nosedive of depression. This was not helped by her smoking habit which she could not break.

They hired some furniture and bought a television for $40. After some rough weeks of adjustment Ray threw himself headlong into his studies. It was hard at the beginning, but as Ray and Lyndie learnt more about faith and the power of God's word they began to put their faith into action. Lyndie was totally delivered from cigarette smoking and they began to experience personal answers to prayer as they learnt to trust God in a new and exciting way.

One day they opened the fridge door to find stark white emptiness staring back at them. They clasped hands and prayed a simple prayer together: 'We thank you Lord for filling our fridge.' At Bible school the following day one of the students came up to Ray and gave him a $100 bill. He told Ray that at a prayer meeting the previous night they had felt constrained to take up an offering for someone who was in need at the school.

They all agreed that the collection should go to Ray and Lyndie. The prayer group had never met the South Africans before, and as Ray and Lyndie were among 1,100 students at the school there was little doubt that this was a very real answer to their simple prayer of faith.

Incidents like this began to challenge Ray, who looks back on those Bible school days as among the most exciting of his life. They were the first small steps in 'living by faith'. Gifts of money and presents arrived from South Africa from time to time, but to help supplement their almost zero income Ray got a job in the one place he knew he would be able to hold his own—a local gymnasium. Even so, his bodybuilding reputation didn't carry much weight when it came to getting a cosy job at the gym. All the owner could offer Ray was a job as a general cleaner. After school Ray would rush to get to work at the gym by one o'clock in the afternoon.

He worked there four days a week, not getting home until well after eleven o'clock at night. In winter it was often nearer one o'clock in the morning before Ray managed to get to bed. He was up again at six o'clock in the morning to study and prepare for the day's lectures, which began at eight o'clock.

Ray's tasks in the gym included cleaning toilets, scrubbing the showers and vacuuming the premises. He was thankful that he had some income. The owner paid him a minimum wage so Ray began to trust God for a promotion—and it came.

By the time Ray was preparing to return to South Africa he was manager of the health spa. The owner was so keen that Ray should stay on in a full-time capacity that he offered him a share in the business and an outrageously high salary to remain in Tulsa. Ray also assisted in opening two health spas in nearby towns, earning some extra pocket money for his advice in setting up the new premises. But, tempting as the offer was, Ray's heart was no longer on material matters. He recognised a calling on his life and was determined to follow that call.

During his stay in Tulsa Ray had the opportunity of witnessing to one of America's famous bodybuilders, Dennis Tinerino. He'd been told that the four-times winner of the Mr Universe title and former Mr America had run foul of the law and was serving a jail sentence in California. The jail sentence was only imposed at night and weekends, allowing the popular sports star to work during the day. Through a mutual friend Ray obtained a telephone number for Tinerino and called him from Tulsa. What followed is best described by Tinerino himself:

'He never gave up calling me on the phone until one day I prayed the sinner's prayer with him. Ray was the most positive, enthusiastic Christian I had ever met in my life. As he shared God's word with me my mind was renewed.

'That night the devil tried to steal God's word from my heart, so I telephoned Ray the next morning. I told him of the battle I was having being in jail, with my marriage and with my finances. Ray said he had a "word" for me from the Lord. He told me, firstly, that I would be released from prison that same night (four months ahead of schedule) and, secondly, the Lord would raise me up and use me for his work.

'That same day my attorney phoned me to tell me that I would be released. I went home and my wife, after first thinking I had escaped from prison, showed me $175,000 worth of bills waiting to be paid. She asked me what I was going to do about the situation. I told her I had a friend in Tulsa who has some high-up connections! I phoned Ray that evening and he told me to put my wife Anita on the line. He told her not to worry about anything.

'Later we flew to Tulsa to meet Ray. Kenneth Hagin prayed for me to receive the baptism of the Holy Spirit. When he did I was thrown bodily off the chair I was sitting on, and couldn't stop talking in tongues for several hours afterwards. From that time God has led me by his Spirit and helped me overcome all my problems. If it had not been for Jesus and his obedient servant, Ray McCauley, I would never have been able to witness to the thousands of people with whom I have shared the gospel.'

The great lessons learnt at Bible school were how to apply the word of God to everyday situations; how to recognise the supernatural and how to use the gifts of the Spirit in a practical way. His studies began to lead him away from the traditional pattern of Christianity which he had followed in the past.

As their studies continued in Tulsa Ray and Lyndie were still unsettled about their future destination. Ray admits that before leaving South Africa there had been a thought at the back of his mind that they would never return to their native land. Because of his close, personal friendship with Kenneth Hagin Jnr he thought there was a possibility of joining the Hagin Ministry, or pastoring a church in America. But three months before they were due to graduate, Ray was sitting in church on a Sunday morning when what he describes as a quiet, inner voice spoke to him, directing him to return to South Africa and pioneer a church.

Lyndie had burst into tears when Ray told her they would be returning to South Africa to start a church! They were tears of joy. She had become homesick and had definite misgivings about staying on in America.

When Ray discussed their decision to return to South Africa with Kenneth Hagin he advised them to start with a service the very first Sunday they arrived back home.

On their return to South Africa Ray followed Hagin's advice and held a service in his parents' home on the first Sunday they were back in the country. Mum and Dad McCauley were thrilled to have their son back and preaching in their own home.

His parents were excited about Ray using the house as a church. Little did they know what they had let themselves in for. The first Sunday meeting drew thirteen people, plus Ray and Lyndie. Ray shared with them the vision that God had given him for the nation. It seemed bombastic and downright presumptuous to hear the way Ray spoke about the future, and how God was going to shake the established religious moulds that existed in South Africa. Yet the next Sunday the lounge was jammed with people and extra chairs were brought in from the kitchen. It was this particular morning that Lyndie's brother Steve was sitting quietly in the service when the Holy Spirit came upon him. Steve, normally very reserved, confounded his sister when he suddenly fell off his chair, began rolling on the carpet and speaking loudly as he received the baptism of the Holy Spirit and spoke in tongues.

The service ended with great excitement in the air. Everyone was so turned on to Jesus that the following week every conceivable floor area was occupied. The McCauleys appealed to people to bring their own chairs because they had already exhausted theirs and their neighbours' supply! So for several weeks the neighbours in Loots Road, in the Randburg suburb of Blairgowrie, stared in amazement as motor cars filled the driveway and the pavement outside the McCauleys' home. Everybody carried a deckchair. What with that, and the joyous shouts of 'Praise the Lord!', neighbours could not be blamed for thinking it was some giant patio party.

Within six weeks it was impossible to continue using his parents' home for church meetings. They had run out of space and the congested parking was bringing complaints from neighbours who did not appreciate being in the middle of a revival. So the search was on for bigger premises.

They found a cinema to let, the Constantia, situated in Tyrwhitt avenue in the suburb of Rosebank. It could seat 600 people. The rent, at the time, seemed exorbitant at R600 (£120) a month. However, they needed a bigger place and the cinema looked ideal. It would also give them plenty of space in which to expand.

After the move to the Constantia cinema the congregation began to grow rapidly, and within three months there were 250 people praising the Lord in the cinema. There were many 'signs and wonders' and some marvellous testimonies of healing were reported. The crowds began to swell, until it was impossible to find a seat, and people began lining the aisles.

6

Opposition

During those early, pioneering days, Ray was looked down upon and heavily criticised by many churchmen. Looking back now, it seems strange that churchmen should have been so critical of the fact that hundreds of people were being won to Christ.

After only eighteen months Ray had to hold three services on Sundays to accommodate the 2,500-strong congregation which packed the Constantia cinema. After a search, they decided to move into the heart of Johannesburg where they were able to hire the 2,000-seater Colosseum cinema. That was in August 1980, and it took off from the very first service.

It was while they were using the Colosseum theatre that Ray felt it was time to look for a more permanent church site, and enquiries were made about buying land. The church caused quite a stir when it showed interest in a property next door to the twenty-one-hectare Brenthurst Estate, which is the home of South Africa's gold and diamond magnate Harry Oppenheimer. In fact, negotiations progressed smoothly for some months as the church consulted with bankers for the purchase of the 3·5 hectare property, Wynford Eagle, formerly the home of millionaire industrialist, the late Mr 'Punch' Barlow. The plan was to restore the baronial-style house on the property and build a 2,000-seater auditorium, as well as a spacious parking area. The property was situated in the wealthy residential suburb of Parktown.

The name Rhema was used for the church now, in line with the spiritual foundations laid at Kenneth Hagin's Rhema Ministries in Tulsa. When the plans became public that the Rhema Church might be moving into such an upper-class locality, the ire of the local Residents' Association was raised and they lodged an objection with the Johannesburg City Council. Their main objection was that few people in the area belonged to Rhema and it 'didn't serve the local community'.

The bankers broke off negotiations and cancelled any further efforts to strike a deal, and Ray and the church board decided not to pursue the matter any further. He felt it wiser to avoid a row, and was having second thoughts anyway about the suitability of the property for the development of the future church.

In November 1980 Ray was told by one of his assistant pastors that there was space to rent in a building in Randburg. He went to look at it and recalls that from the moment he saw the building he knew that God wanted him to buy it. The building at that time housed a supermarket, a furniture store and a bakery. It was owned by a Mr Tony Factor, a highly successful business tycoon. Ray felt that the building would be ideal, not only for a large auditorium, but also to house a bookshop, a Bible Training Centre and administrative offices.

Mr Factor, a likable, volatile personality, who had introduced discount furniture stores into South Africa, always kept a high publicity profile. At one stage of his business career he even began discounting coffins, much to the chagrin of the nation's undertakers, who protested that his discounting would be the death knell of funeral parlours!

When Factor heard that Ray wanted to buy his building and convert it into a church he couldn't believe he was serious. His gravel-voiced reply to Ray was simple: 'There's no church with that kind of money to buy my property.' Tony, a Jew, held a view shared by many businessmen (Jew or Gentile) that churches were mostly poverty-stricken, always having cake sales to raise money for building funds. For the first time in his life, Tony got another view of Christianity.

After several more telephone calls and meetings a deal was struck and signed. Rhema agreed to buy the property for R2·2-million (about half a million pounds) and lease back a small area of the warehouse to Tony Factor. When the deal was signed Rhema agreed to pay a cash amount of R50,000 by a certain date. When agreeing to this clause Ray knew they did not have the full amount in the bank. He was convinced that God had directed him in the deal, confidently believing the money would arrive in time for the payment.

The amount was due on a Monday. On the Friday before the deadline Tony Factor enquired whether Ray had the money. Ray simply replied: 'The Lord will provide.' To which Tony countered: 'Yes, I know the Lord provides, but where will *you* get the money?' The answer came at the Sunday service at the Colosseum Cinema. Included in the offering was a brown paper packet. In it was R25,000, which was sufficient to put together with what they had in the bank.

The next day when Ray presented the R50,000 cheque to Tony Factor, the discount king almost fell off his leather chair. And so Rhema had a permanent home, at least for the next four years. The premises were refurbished. An auditorium seating 2,500 people was laid out, with the podium in the centre. On March 23, 1981, Kenneth Hagin Snr led a packed congregation in a dedication service, in which he commented, significantly, 'This is only the beginning.'

The church remained in the converted warehouse for four years. Growth in all areas continued, and a decision was made to find a large tract of land and build a complex that could cope with the continued expansion. A site was found on a gentle slope in the Randpark Ridge area of Randburg, only a ten-minute drive away from the present church. The site was situated in a fairly new residential area. This fact gave them confidence that there would not be any serious objections from home-owners in the immediate vicinity.

Sadly, however, a bitter row did develop, but on this occasion Ray did not back down. From the beginning he believed that God had destined the property for the new church complex. Indeed, it took a miracle to purchase it, because it turned out that the property was actually three separate lots, owned by three different parties. The negotiations were highly confidential and delicate because if one party got an inkling of the proposed deal, they could have held out for a much bigger amount. With professional skill Rhema bought the 13 hectares of prime land for the remarkably low sum of R230,000.

That, in fact, proved the easiest part of the deal, because very shortly after that the local residents were in full cry, petitioning the town council and taking legal opinion. They were determined to stop the building of the Rhema Church.

The building saga began in November 1982. It was the beginning of a three-year battle which was waged by the Ratepayers' Association and fanned by a stream of critical letters which continually filled the pages of the local newspapers.

The tentative plan was to construct an auditorium which would seat 10,000 people and, of course, a huge parking area. In addition there would be a Bible Training Centre, a Children's Church, an administrative block, and a wholesale and retail book and tape outlet on site.

The first salvo in the battle was fired in the weekly newspaper the *Randburg Sun*. In December 1983, under the headline 'RESIDENTS CONCERNED OVER PLANS FOR HYPER-CHURCH', the reporter said that residents of Ward 11 planned to see the Director of Local Government. Fears, expressed by local residents, mainly centred on their concern for the 'tranquillity of the environment'. One ratepayer pointed out that Rhema was not a 'once-a-week-church'. There would be comings and goings every day and residents would lose their privacy.

The residents were assured by Rhema that the building and landscaping of the site would enhance the area. Neither would they be inconvenienced in any way by the new super-church. The residents, however, were not satisfied with these assurances. They continued to lobby support either to stop the conversion of the property for church rights, or to restrict the capacity of the auditorium to 1,000 people only.

The church pressed on with the project, and eventually in June 1983 the Randburg Management Board gave the go-ahead for the building of the complex, with the strict proviso that the auditorium seating be restricted to 5,000 people only.

The ratepayers were still on the warpath, extremely unhappy with the prospect of having a 5,000-seater

Ray enjoys preaching

church in their area. A petition, with almost 1,000 names on it, was whipped up in an attempt to block the church.

Ray refused to be intimidated by the very vocal Ratepayers' Association. Although final permission from the provincial authorities had not yet been received for the changing of the property rights to ecclesiastical rights, Ray and the Church Building Committee decided to go ahead and put the project out for tender.

With consent already granted by the town council it was highly unlikely that the provincial authorities would override their decision. It was regarded as a mere formality. This permission was given, but remained a point of contention and a lever which the opponents to the church used over the next twelve months.

Once the tenders had been accepted, the first phase began with the preparation of the ground. Huge earthmoving equipment lumbered onto the property, much to the annoyance of the Ratepayers' Association, who doggedly continued to snipe at Rhema. Despite the complaints the final approval for the building complex came through from the provincial authorities in April 1984. The building went ahead, and on June 16, 1985, the impressive new Rhema Bible Church complex was dedicated to the Lord. The main speaker was Kenneth Hagin.

As part of the big day an elaborate musical presentation by the Rhema band set the stage for the dedication. Ray, hardly a man to fuss about special occasions, played a low-key role in the course of the day. In fact, he acted as usher for a while as thousands of people tried to get into the already packed auditorium. The doors had to be closed two hours before the official starting time.

The media attended the impressive opening ceremony and a daily morning newspaper *The Citizen* recorded:

'The pale blue auditorium was filled with song as believers celebrated Pastor Ray McCauley's triumph—the opening of the biggest church building on the African continent.'

7

Making News

Now with a permanent home, the Rhema Church steadily began to increase its influence in the nation. Ray acquired a high public profile and was a constant target for the media. However, he and the church were merely seen as unorthodox controversialists, who could not have any lasting impact upon the socio-political pattern of the country.

The attraction of the newspapers for Ray, though, was not that surprising. While he was a star bodybuilder he attracted media coverage—even more so when he accepted Jesus Christ as his Saviour in 1969. From the outset of his bodybuilding exploits, and later when he owned his own health studios, Ray saw the value of publicity and cultivated a lot of goodwill for himself with the pressmen of Johannesburg.

One of them was Mervyn Rees, one of South Africa's finest investigative journalists, who got to know Ray when he first met him in a gymnasium. Rees and Ray became good friends, so that when the reporter started an in-depth investigation into the sordid drug scene in the city, Ray was the first to offer his help—as a bodyguard!

Rees recalls: 'When I told him I was doing the rounds of the dingy nightspots of the city, probably meeting with some dangerous characters, Ray immediately volunteered his help if I had problems with any thugs. "You just let me know if you have any trouble and I'll sort it out for you," he told me.'

During those early years Rees featured Ray in several stories, and still has a photograph of Ray with a very young Arnold Schwarzenegger who visited South Africa in the early seventies. Rees, now an international correspondent, was one of the few journalists who put aside the news media's usual cynicism when it came to assessing Ray's success as a churchman. He saw Ray as a genuine young man always willing to help. 'I never saw any malice in him. He was always open and honest.'

That image with the media began to alter when Ray and Lyndie returned from Tulsa. Up to his departure for Tulsa in 1978 Ray had undoubtedly enjoyed a more than favourable and fair press in South Africa. It changed on his return to Johannesburg in 1979.

He was no longer a champion bodybuilder doing good among schoolchildren and youth groups. He was now a preacher, an ordained minister of the gospel. His educational background, once ignored by the media, now became a focus of ridicule, mentioned time and again over the next few years.

The media, it seemed, were unwilling to accept that an ex-Mr Universe finalist, with a standard eight education, was qualified to preach the gospel. They assumed that he was in it for the money! But it was not only this transformation which caused the press to target their pens on Ray. On his return from studying in Tulsa, Ray immediately began preaching a gospel message that was powerfully positive when measured against some traditional preaching. It was, in fact, the negative reaction of some churches which gave the media the ammunition to start sniping at the new Rhema Church.

The crucial areas of controversy were the teaching on divine healing and biblical prosperity. Even today these are pillars of debate within the church. Ray's absolute commitment to the word of God marked him as a radical preacher. Attempts were made to brand him a cultist. One can excuse the media for their lack of insight into the intricate vagaries of Christian doctrine. However, it was a sad reflection on many churchmen, because it was mainly their vendetta which produced such negative publicity.

Incredible stories have been supposedly 'leaked' to the press, one being that Ray has a secret bank account in Switzerland. Other gossips claim that Ray forced people to pay him after praying for them. One day a well-known friend of Ray's was sitting with two lawyers and heard the one say to the other: 'Do you know that Ray McCauley lays hands on Porsches. He charges R400 a time and the cars never give any trouble.'

Regrettably, these unfounded and ridiculous rumours poisoned many media men, some of whom even today believe Ray is a charlatan. In fairness to the media, there is no doubt that Ray has been 'good copy'. The phenomenal growth of the church from a handful in 1979 to over 16,000 members in 1992, has been staggering.

Unfortunately, the media have been unable to grasp the spiritual value of this religious awakening in South Africa, which involves not only the Rhema Church but many other movements across the country. From the beginning of the Rhema ministry, Ray had a prominent public image because his approach to church was, to say the least, different when compared with traditionalists. The congregation grew at a prodigious rate. So it was only logical that with such a big following large amounts of finance would be generated from tithing and Sunday offerings.

Rhema also sells thousands of audio cassettes, Christian books and videos. All of these products yield added finance. Even a casual observer could not help notice that the Rhema Church was generating large amounts of money. This gnawed at the public's curiosity.

Rhema's outward image was one of materialism, especially when contrasted with the customary parish priest, who so often correlated lack of wealth to supposed spiritual well-being. This so-called 'prosperity message' drew even greater media attention. The teaching brought fierce and caustic condemnation from an array of church leaders. It caused Rhema to be labelled a 'prosperity cult', a connotation which the media latched onto, especially when they heard about huge offerings collected at church services. Some assumed Ray was banking these offerings in his own personal account, failing to appreciate that he was subject to a Church Board that set his salary.

Despite attempts to explain, the press refused to listen, sure that they were on to one of the biggest con artists of the century. In the pursuit of the highest standards of journalism reporters vied with one another in an effort to clinch the great exposé story. So after an Afrikaans Sunday newspaper series was completed on 'faith healing', the mass-selling *Sunday Times* jumped on the religion bandwagon when they launched a probe into what was dubbed the 'God Industry'.

This supposedly objective probe was further encouraged by a study done by Professor Lawrence Schlemmer and Mrs Elda Morran, of the Natal University's Centre for Applied Social Sciences for Diakonia, which represents many of the traditional churches in the greater Durban area. The study, which claimed to have taken a year to complete, echoed the antagonism and resentment that certain religious leaders had adopted towards Ray and the hundreds of independent churches which were springing up all around the country.

In part of its conclusion the study said: 'In Christian terms, the doctrinal foundation of the new churches can be shown to be incorrect, if not heretical. The fundamentally manipulative attitude towards God, embodied in the prosperity message, can be shown to be contrary to the very basis of Christian faith.'

It was the reference to the controversial prosperity message which caught the interest of the *Sunday Times* reporter, who like so many newspaper journalists hoped once and for all that she would be able to expose Ray and others in the new spiritual awakening as nothing but a bunch of rogues, whose only real interest was in emptying the pockets of the unsuspecting congregations.

Although the earlier Afrikaans newspaper investigation had centred on healing, its main intention had been to try and prove that the new-wave 'faith' churches, spearheaded by Rhema, were linked to financial gain, and that men like Ray and others were making the public pay before praying for them.

The newspaper could not in any way substantiate these inferences. However, the jingle of the cash register at Rhema fascinated the media and intrigued the general public. So when the *Sunday Times* launched its investigation into the 'God Industry' it zeroed in on the financial aspect. The opening paragraph of the first series of articles set the tone. It read:

> In an economy ravaged by recession, enormous profits are being reaped by a new breed of entrepreneur—the faith peddlers.

The article went on to quote a Roman Catholic theologian, who was reported as saying: 'They're making a business out of religion.' A prominent leader of the Methodist Church added, 'These churches use supermarket strategy.' He went on to ask 'whether this is the authentic gospel'. He damned the notion that health and wealth were 'purely the consequences of faith'.

The series of articles continued with a non-stop attack on the so-called 'faith movement', sensationalising accounts from a couple of disillusioned ex-Rhema adherents. It was a typical newspaper tactic of highlighting a minority, dissident voice and ignoring the silent majority.

To the gullible and uninformed general public it was what they wanted to read, confirming the wild rumours they had heard about Ray, Rhema and the new-wave faith churches. The *Sunday Times* letters pages were splashed with replies for and against. At least some people were not shaken by the 'God Industry' series.

In the end the newspaper articles failed to 'expose' any malpractices concerning money—which had been the main thrust of the reports. Many casual readers wrote and telephoned in to tell Ray how much they abhorred the personal attacks which were levelled against him. They all felt that it was an unwarranted personal vendetta.

The newspaper series, unfortunately, deeply divided the body of Christ, and more seeds of doubt were sown about the authenticity of the Rhema revival and the prosperity message in South Africa. While this controversy was raging in the press, one of the city's biggest auditing companies had just completed an audit on the Rhema books. Their comment on the books was that they were among the best kept and most orderly set of financial records they had come across. In fact, they went so far as to say that it had been a privilege to audit their books! This fact was never reported by the press.

The constant media debate, involving prosperity, healing and the marathon battle with the local Ratepayers' Association in Randburg, placed tremendous pressure on Ray and Lyndie. Even when the building project was under way Ray faced further criticism as to why R7 million (£1·4 million) was being spent on a church building and not given to feed the poor. This became the parroted question of every reporter in town for several weeks. The pressure and range of accusations took their toll. After one particular interview with a reporter, Lyndie burst into tears on her husband's shoulder. She had been so distressed at the way the reporter had attacked Ray.

Ray's response was to lock himself in his study and, as he put it, have a moan about the media before the Lord. He's admitted that he almost felt like crying out for bolts of lightning to strike down every journalist in town!

Ray considered engaging a public relations company to improve the Rhema image. It was shelved because, after consideration, it was thought it would have been impossible for a secular PR firm to grasp the spiritual affairs of a church or the move of God in South Africa.

On my advice Ray gave a very frank and straight interview to a Johannesburg *Sunday Star* reporter Anne Quayle. I chanced to meet this reporter during an earlier controversy over healing. Claims of divine healing had led Mrs Quayle to cover the religious 'beat' and she told me some horrendous stories which ostensibly involved Ray and members of Rhema.

As a result I arranged for Mrs Quayle, who described herself as a lapsed Roman Catholic, to have an eyeball-to-eyeball interview with Ray—no holds barred. There was one condition: that the *Sunday Star* printed the answers to the allegations. The interview was conducted amid the builders, dust and rubble of the site of the new Rhema Ministries' headquarters.

Mrs Quayle, as she admitted during the interview, played devil's advocate. Beside a barrage of questions about healing and miracles, there was the now familiar jibes about finances. In a frankness which amazed the reporter, Ray breezed his way through this minefield of criticism.

Thus Ray convinced at least one hardened reporter that he was a genuine, warm-hearted man. Ray's classic quote of the interview was: 'Either this is the world's greatest con, or it's from God,' which produced the banner headline the next Sunday morning: 'IT'S A CON, OR IT'S GOD'. This refreshing interview seemed to soften the attitude of other newspaper reporters. Even the *Sunday Times*, which always appeared to be in the vanguard of the attempts at character assassination, decided that they would need to give some preview coverage to the opening and dedication of the new church.

They sent reporter Cas St Leger, who had in the 'God Industry' series written some rather unpalatable things about Ray. Cas and a photographer arrived on a Friday morning as the builders were engaged in last-minute finishing touches to the vast auditorium.

Ray spotted the two of them and, because of his previous dealings with the reporter, tried to make a run for cover. He admitted to me that he really didn't want to speak to the reporter again, not after the misquotes and factual errors which had been published before. However, he was too slow—Cas St Leger nailed him. I stood nearby wondering whether Ray would explode and castigate her. What he did absolutely confounded the reporter—and the photographer, who looked on wide-eyed. He opened his arms to hug her, and greeted her with a warm Christian salutation, a practical demonstration of walking in love, and turning the other cheek.

I know it took a hefty chunk of humility to make that open and friendly approach to the reporter whose sole aim up to that point had been to crucify him if she could, but it made an impression. The welcome she had received was written up in her report the next Sunday. Of course, the headline writers still had their dig with 'THE PICK AND PRAY HYPER-CHURCH', but although it offended some it brought a smile to Ray's face.

The positive media attitude continued for several months, with events fairly covered by both the newspapers and television, including Ray's meeting with the then President, Mr P. W. Botha, and other members of the South African Government.

There was one nasty incident which was again reported by the *Sunday Times*. Reporter Cas St Leger was again the villain of the piece, although unwittingly one assumes. The real initiator was once again a churchman. The reporter gained access to a document by a Presbyterian theologian which berated Ray and Rhema Ministries. It was unbelievably vitriolic and branded him a heretic and false prophet. With great glee in her voice Cas St Leger telephoned me in an attempt to get Ray to respond to this vicious attack. When I called her back with Ray's comment she was audibly startled. His official reply was simply this: 'It is my policy and that of Rhema Ministries South Africa, not to criticise any other church or denomination, but to strive to work in unity with all Christians, especially at this time in our country.'

Cas St Leger's surprise at this reply to the hatchet job that the theologian was trying to do on Rhema, was audible on the other end of the telephone. She spluttered out: 'But how can Ray make such a comment . . . just think if it was the other way around . . . the Presbyterians would come back with everything.' I repeated the statement that Ray had given me, and told her that there was no malice involved. If she had to write the story, all that Ray wanted published was his comment as I had transmitted it to her. Bewildered, she put down the telephone. The story duly appeared with the headline emphasis, of course, on the heresy. Ray's reply was tacked on the end, and to any mature Christian who read the article, the last paragraph deflated the whole claim.

There was a sequel to the story when the Presbyterian Assembly twice voted against their theologian's report. This was reported prominently by one newspaper, although the *Sunday Times* chose to ignore this rebuff to their original story and headline.

Within a few days Ray received a personal letter from a senior Presbytery official, who apologised on behalf of the denomination for the unfortunate attack. He shared their denomination's support and prayers for the work that Rhema was doing in South Africa. Another letter, from a group of Presbyterian women from an assembly in the suburb of Edenvale, also reached Ray. The writer of the letter, an elder in the church, told how they had met at an early morning prayer meeting and had asked forgiveness on behalf of those who had been responsible for the scathing attack on Ray and Rhema. They added how much they appreciated the ministry of their fellow Christian brother.

Undoubtedly, Ray believes in the power of the media. He has been willing to run the risk of being caught in the crossfire of sensationalism. His heartfelt desire is to see the media of South Africa acknowledge Jesus Christ as Lord. They sometimes do. Like the occasion when reporter Winnie Graham came across a human interest story that touched her heart. She decided to record it in the November 7, 1985 issue of the *Randburg Sun*. She wrote:

For one reason or another Rhema's Pastor Ray McCauley has not always been the most popular man in Randburg. When his church built its new headquarters in Rand Park Ridge controversy raged—only to die quietly when the residents in the area realised Rhema churchgoers were not as noisy as they thought they would be. It is perhaps because he has had a fairly difficult time—gaining acceptance from Randburg ratepayers—that I would like to tell this story about Ray.

A Black housewife I know from Soweto told me last week that the turmoil in the area had finally got to her. For months unrest had flared in other parts of the sprawling township, but it had not touched her area. Then—just last week—she awoke to be told a man had been murdered in her street in the early hours of the morning. The entire area was in a ferment.

Then came worse news: a schoolboy she knew was killed in reprisal later that day. 'I was feeling pretty depressed. I went to work and came home again, but the tension in my street remained. The telephone rang and a friend asked if I had heard the Revd Ray McCauley would be preaching in the Dube Hall that evening. She wanted me to come with her.'

The women had no transport, but managed to find a taxi,

and off they went to Dube. It turned out to be a memorable experience. The hall was packed to capacity. Young and old wanted to hear what Pastor McCauley had to say. He was not to disappoint them.

'He used Psalm 91 as the basis of his sermon. And what a comfort it brought us—especially when he told us that we had God's total protection. He said God would look after us in Soweto. If we believed in Him there was no need to fear the arrows by day or the terror by night.'

The anguish she had felt earlier in the day left her, she said, but what made her happier was the reaction of the congregation. The young people of Soweto, who have carried much of the blame for the unrest, were well represented.

Ray's message of hope had them crying out 'Thank you, Jesus' and 'Praise the Lord'. The Rhema band joined them in music and song. A total of thirty-nine people went forward wanting to be 'reborn'. Afterwards, the woman told me, Pastor McCauley moved among the crowd shaking hands, hugging people and telling all: 'God loves you. I love you.' Then he invited them to have tea and sandwiches with him before going home well after 9 pm. The Black housewife was pleased and surprised that a White pastor had the courage to visit Soweto at a time when the township was in turmoil. His visit was unmarked by incident.

It was a heartwarming story, especially when viewed against the backdrop of violence and racism being splashed in the media around the world. This report never made international headlines.

There were a few other successes in the early days when in mid-June 1985 Ray appeared on the SABC television programme *Eyeline*. He was interviewed by astute and professional media man Pat Rogers. The interview was pre-taped and advertised for viewing on a Thursday night.

At 5 o'clock on the Thursday evening Rogers was told

the McCauley interview was to be replaced by a hastily prepared substitute programme. No explanation or new date was given for the airing of the interview.

The SABC authorities, however, did not take into account the reaction of hundreds of Christians around the country, who bombarded the TV headquarters at Auckland Park with telephone calls demanding to know why the McCauley interview was cancelled at the last moment. The SABC TV hierarchy bowed to pressure and a new programme was recorded and transmitted. Ray was at his smiling best for the interview. There's no doubt that he has a relaxing, personal charm and flashing smile that immediately disarms.

Pat Rogers, who always did his homework before an interview, had a couple of loaded questions which he hoped would trip Ray up. However, Ray parried well and walked out of the studio with a halo hovering over his head. . . .

The newspaper critics also saw the programme. The Johannesburg evening newspaper the *Star* had this comment to make about the interview:

Has Pat Rogers lost his grip, I ask? Or is he just uncomfortable with a subject that encompasses religion? 'I'm not going to ask you how much you earn!' says our Pat too sweetly for words. 'No, otherwise I'll ask you how much you earn,' retorts Ray.

It would have taken a very much more hardened interviewer to faze the pastor—that was obvious. He came over as positively incorruptible and twice as sincere. He even managed a moderately sensible answer to the incredible question about raising the dead or walking on water . . . McCauley smiled indulgently and took it all in his stride, murmuring something about the power of medicine.

It was a little unfair, I thought, of Rogers to save all the 'juicy details' till the closing moments, revealing McCauley's past (which didn't seem all murky, anyway) and offering him a few minutes—no seconds—to explain himself. Bit below the belt, that was, not that McCauley needed any help.

Anyway, how can you hold a hard-hitting interview with someone who is so smilingly nice? In the end 'Eyeline' became a glorious advertisement for the new Rhema Church. Under the circumstances, I wouldn't have thought it needed advertising, but good luck to it and Ray McCauley. One thing's for sure, that one ain't stupid.

Another television critic, on the *Pretoria News* newspaper included this snippet in his column:

This week's Golden Naartjie Award nomination goes to 'Eyeline'. It was a marvellous interview with Pastor Ray McCauley, of the Rhema Church, in which the interviewer seemed unsure whether to praise or to attack him. In the end Pastor McCauley 'hijacked' the interview and gave himself, the Rhema Church and his accountants a jolly good plug.

8

Racial Conflict

From the birth of the church in 1979 until about 1985 Rhema rode the seas of controversy caused by wrong perceptions and a preponderance of negative public exposure. Yet, despite all the media negativity, the church grew—in fact it was an explosion. Rhema, whether people liked it or not, had arrived on the church map. Its sheer size, affluence (a point of major criticism) and growing influence made it a phenomenon that could not be ignored.

The task of overseeing such a work is in itself demanding, and Ray could have ignored any outside socio-political involvement of the church and continued with the building of Rhema and its congregation. In the first five or six years he certainly didn't show much inclination to express a political opinion or to make any meaningful comment on political events from the pulpit, unlike men like Bishop Desmond Tutu and others who in the eighties were continually in the glare of the media as they boldly attacked the South African Government on the morality of apartheid.

Yet factors were at work in the Rhema Church which were to reshape much of Ray's apolitical thinking. Although believing itself to be politically neutral, Rhema, from its inception, had been founded on a non-racial basis, and its membership open to all people of all races. Without realising it fully, the church had already made a so-called political statement—it was against apartheid.

Most churches and certainly Pentecostal denominations were strictly segregated into the four main racial components—Black, White, Coloured, and Indian. At Rhema no such distinction was followed. Because the Government had relaxed certain apartheid laws it was possible for non-White people to attend so-called 'White-only' churches.

As Rhema grew it attracted a sizable number of Black, Coloured and Indian followers, and as they became active members of the church they felt a freedom to challenge Ray on a few issues. One of these was the flying of the South African flag. Influenced partially by the patriotic spirit of the Americans and the ostentatious display of the Stars and Stripes at churches he had seen in the USA, Ray had decided to give the national flag some prominence. Mini-pennants appeared on desks, and when Rhema dedicated its new church complex, South African flags flapped in the wind from the top of specially erected masts. To the average White member of the congregation it really meant very little. To Blacks, including Christians, who were becoming more and more politically motivated, the South African flag spoke of only one thing—oppression.

After listening to the views of a Black deputation Ray decided to take the flags down and to ban any official display in the church. So the flags went and hardly any of the White members knew about the rumpus.

The flag incident may seem insignificant, yet it is something which has repeatedly haunted the church and been referred to by liberal-minded critics of Rhema. In numerous research papers and booklets published in South Africa and overseas, the flying of the national flag has been used as proof of Rhema's so-called support of the Government and apartheid.

Because of the extraordinary growth of Rhema and the so-called 'faith message' university sociologists became interested in the movement and the people involved in it. For reasons that only these researchers can explain most of their papers seemed to go out of their way to make political statements and seemingly deliberate attempts to isolate Rhema as a bunch of misdirected zealots who believed in apartheid.

The flag issue, then, was probably Ray's first deliberate political decision, and it made him more sensitive to the Black situation and determined to examine the implications of the gospel in relationship to apartheid.

Following up his resolve to oppose racial discrimination where and when he could, without resorting to simple rhetoric and media hype, Ray decided he would never speak at a venue which was racially segregated. This decision came after he had been 'tricked' into speaking at a hall in the town of Rustenburg, a hotbed of conservative-minded people who believe in rigid, racial segregation. Not realising that the hall was for Whites only, Ray preached there and only at the end of the service when some Black people tried to respond to an altar call did it dawn on him that the Black people had not been allowed inside the hall. After that incident he firmly resolved not to preach there again—unless it was to a multi-racial congregation.

Slowly, Ray was being initiated into the milieu of religion and politics. He also began to realise that to have any credibility and right to a say in the life of the nation meant getting involved in pertinent socio-political issues. One of the strengths of Ray's preaching is its relevancy to day-to-day life. Now even more so, he began to see the need to make the gospel relevant in the socio-political arena of South Africa.

Many godly men had given prophetic utterances over Ray, going back to 1979, and a common thread was always a role for Ray in the life of the nation. For these prophecies to come to pass he had to do more than just sit and wait—he had to make a decision to stand up and be counted. That meant an application of the word of God to political moral issues, entailing some radical rethinking.

Another reason which caused Ray to get embroiled in the realities of apartheid was education. Part of the vision for the church was Christian education. It became rather ironic that Ray, with only a standard eight certificate, became the president of the nationwide network of Christian schools which mushroomed throughout the country.

Rhema started its own school, which because it was a private school and received no State subsidy was allowed to admit children of all races. This was, in general, the policy throughout the network of independent churches which had blossomed in every town and city since 1979. Although permitted to run a multi-racial, private school, a minefield of apartheid laws often thwarted the practice of a racially integrated school. This happened to a sister church and school situated in the industrial complex of the Vaal Triangle in the town of Vereeniging.

The pastor of Kingdom Ministries, Mark Blatt,

telephoned to speak urgently to Ray one day to inform him that the Vereeniging Town Council was threatening to close down his school. The reason was the presence of Black pupils in an area and building which was reserved for Whites only. Blatt, a pugnacious person when it came to standing for the gospel, was rallying support to fight the council in the law courts. Ray gave him his blessing; that was the beginning of a prolonged legal struggle.

The Member of Parliament for Vereeniging at the time was Mr F. W. de Klerk, who gave the impression of not wanting to get involved in the schools row, but watched the battle with keen interest and obviously admired the stand taken by the school. In December of that year, Ray, on holiday at his seaside home on the Natal south coast, received a telephone call from Mr de Klerk, wishing him well over the festive season. Ray was surprised at receiving the call from Mr de Klerk, because up to then he had never met or spoken to him.

The Kingdom School row eventually reached the Supreme Court in Pretoria, and on the day of the verdict Ray joined Mark Blatt and his team of lawyers in the courtroom.

The verdict handed down slammed the Vereeniging Town Council and they lost the case and were ordered to pay the Kingdom School's cost which amounted to over R100,000 (£20,000). There was much jubilation and thanksgiving to the Lord for this important legal victory over racism. The precedent it set could well be used in future cases where town council authorities attempted to justify racism by hiding behind outdated and antiquated laws.

The Kingdom School issue further baptised Ray into some of the harsh realities of apartheid South Africa. Like tens of thousands of other Whites Ray, although instinctively knowing the wrongs of racism, had up to then hardly done anything concrete to oppose or to end the evil system.

The triumphs of the Supreme Court ruling were tempered a few months later when the State educational authorities began an intense investigation of the Christian schools which were flourishing across the land. This expansion of Christian schools was made possible by the introduction of the 'Accelerated Christian Education' (ACE) programme, an American system which did away with conventional classrooms and minimised the number of teachers required, relying heavily on the pupils learning from specially prepared books. The concept appealed to many churches who were displeased with the State-run schools because of declining teaching standards and an alarming growth of occult practices which were being reported from schools across the country.

The relative ease with which a school could be organised by simply employing a couple of teachers, buying the required set books and using any spare room that was available, made it attractive to churches large and small. Within a short while seventy ACE schools were up and running.

However, there were serious flaws in the system, and some churches abused the scheme by providing inadequate classroom space and sometimes hiring unqualified staff. The State authorities moved against the ACE schools by threatening to shut down half of them, unless certain criteria were attained.

The first reaction of the school principals and churches was that of annoyance at the Government's interference. There was some hint that the real reason for the Government blitz of the ACE schools was their multi-racial nature. Although this was later denied it is hard not to believe that it was one of the elements which caused the Government to act against the schools.

Ray was brought into the row by virtue of being the President of ACE in South Africa. He ordered an internal investigation of the schools and was appalled when it was discovered that many of the Government's allegations were true. However, fault was also found on the Government's side, which in some cases had failed to communicate with schools for over a year.

The authorities, however, would not budge on a deadline they had set, which caused consternation and confusion to hundreds of parents and pupils who did not know where they would be going to school in the new term. It was decided to seek an urgent meeting with the Government minister in charge of education.

The meeting took place in Government offices in Cape Town with the Minister of National Education Mr Piet Claase. Ray led a four-man delegation, which flew down for an afternoon meeting with the cabinet minister. I was in the delegation to handle the media.

The schools row was major news in almost every national and country newspaper because it seemed that almost every town, large or small, had an ACE school. As a result they came under the media spotlight. The public debate had got quite heated and hardly a day went by without some newspaper telephoning me for an update on the situation. Statements and counter statements, press conferences and television debates raged, so when the meeting was arranged in Cape Town the ACE delegation wanted to make sure it got a fair say in the press.

The meeting was set for after lunch and lasted for nearly two hours. Minister Claase was flanked by senior officials of the educational body, and as the debate developed I could not help smiling to myself. Here was

Ray, his best academic achievement a standard eight certificate, in heated discussion with highly erudite educational authorities, on the virtues of different learning systems.

Despite a certain amount of dogmatism on the side of the educational authorities Minister Claase and Ray managed a compromise which allowed ACE schools an extended time limit to meet certain requirements as set by the authorities.

Then followed several months of haggling, but a solution was ultimately forged. Some schools were forced to close their doors, because they could not reach the required standard, but when the dust had settled sixty out of eighty schools were operative and all seemed to be going smoothly.

Then, with the emergence of more radical Right Wing political activists, another school row flared, this time in Brits, a small predominantly Afrikaner town, situated about two hours' drive north-west of Johannesburg. The issue this time was not educational, but racial.

A local pastor, Peter Varrie, established a church and decided that a school was needed because of the inadequate facilities available, especially for Black children. The intrepid Peter Varrie went ahead with a building and soon had a full house of pupils, mainly Black. From the start of the project he was warned by the local town council that they would take action against him. Varrie accepted the challenge.

The predicament for Varrie was the fact that the Brits town council was controlled by the Right-Wing Conservative Party, which were avowed separatists and dedicated to keeping apartheid alive. When Ray heard about the clash he gave his full backing to Varrie and authorised me to orchestrate a media campaign—if it was needed. Although some minor media coverage was obtained, appeals were made by all parties concerned, including a highly-placed security policeman, for the matter to be resolved without sensationalising the issue in the press.

Reluctantly we agreed, despite great provocation from the Brits Town Council, which tried to intimidate Varrie and the teachers by cutting off the electricity and threatening eviction. The tougher the opposition got the more resolute Varrie became, with Ray determined to support him all the way, even if it meant going to the Supreme Court again.

Ignoring the threats and intimidation Varrie continued to run the school, hiring a portable power plant to provide electricity. He then invited Ray to a special opening and dedication ceremony. It was on a Friday night. Ray set off wondering whether he might find a lynching mob waiting to disrupt the service.

The hall was jam-packed with over 600 people, representing parents of pupils as well as many of the townfolk. Ray pulled no punches with a hard-hitting message that addressed the issue of living out one's Christianity. He directly challenged people who tried to justify racist actions with Christian beliefs. He got a rousing reception.

Since then there have been a few minor incidents, but the school is now firmly established and a community which brands itself, politically, as racist, is learning to be tolerant of people of other colour. Such are the incongruities of South Africa.

During 1990 the matter of education came more and more under the national spotlight because of the dire need to upgrade Black education and maintain adequate standards of learning. Several major political decisions were made during the year, some of which entailed 'privatising' so-called White Government schools which had been closed down. Referenda were held in schools across the country to seek attitudes towards integrating Blacks into the previously 'Whites-only' structure.

As Ray viewed the changes, there was a certain satisfaction in his heart that it had indeed been God who had urged him and others to make the move nearly five years previously to start multi-racial Christian schools. While the State system was only beginning to tackle the problem, the church was well on its way to providing tomorrow's leaders, not only with a sound academic training but with solid Christian foundations.

By 1990 Ray openly confessed that his whole way of thinking had been radically changed on the issue of racism, and that he had been patently naive in not recognising the linkage between social responsibility, the gospel and the wrongs of apartheid.

What effect did this have on the congregation? In general they applauded, although some White members may have thought he was getting 'too involved in politics'. The reaction from Black members was not as jubilant as Ray presumed. They expected him to become more and more radical and champion the Black cause and so-called liberation struggle with greater enthusiasm. Ray was wary of falling into that trap. He realised that he trod a dangerous path, that his priority was to preach the gospel. Although willing to speak out on social issues and get involved on a practical level, he appreciated the necessity for neutrality in the political field.

Since 1979 Ray has doggedly tried to live by the word of God, submitting personal views and opinions to its final authority. As he has sought enlightenment from the Bible on the matters of civil government and social matters, he has followed the same principle of doing what the Bible declares.

Such a position sometimes sounds corny, because most

Christians would agree, broadly, that they endeavour to submit their lives to the word of God. In the context of South Africa it sometimes sounds hypocritical, especially to non-Christians. After all, was not the Dutch Reformed Church following Scripture when it supported apartheid?

As the struggle for a New South Africa unfolds, the Bible is again being brandished by a large segment of Afrikaners as their blueprint and reason for demanding a separate State for Whites, only because they refuse to allow themselves to be ruled by Blacks. Like many previous conflicts in world history, each party is claiming that God is on its side. The ANC-Communist Party alliance has made good profit out of extolling the virtues of Liberation Theology.

Ray, in his biblical beliefs, tries to be as balanced as possible, avoiding the extremes of Right-Wing or Left-Wing theology. This makes him a strange hybrid in view of his fundamentalist doctrine and his broadening socio-political theology.

In a way Ray, like other concerned churchmen, is attempting to straddle the chasms that exist in the religious, political, social, cultural and tribal extremes of South Africa. In a nation divided into so many camps, Ray and other church leaders are seeing more and more that the only possible common denominator must be the Bible. Yet to be relevant he must avoid being labelled or boxed into any specific political, religious, racial, or cultural grouping.

To achieve this end has meant trying to shake off some of the preconceived stereotypes and, just as important, building bridges and making new contacts, especially within the vast church family. To win recognition from the Christian family of churches has not been easy. The church family often regards Rhema as an ugly duckling (by the theologians) or as a delinquent child. Trying to gain the nod of approval from the churches has been difficult, from all angles.

Despite being Pentecostal, the denominational tongue-talkers gave Rhema much verbal criticism, while the evangelicals stood aloof and the traditionalists looked at the 'toddlers' throwing sand at each other and wondered when the Pentecostal part of the family would ever get any semblance of respectability.

9

Leading the Way

Two essential ingredients in establishing Ray's credibility as an influential national leader have been his role in two church organisations.

In 1982 a loose fellowship of some prominent leaders in the new spiritual awakening in South Africa began. It was initiated by pastor Ed Roebert, of the Hatfield Community Church in Pretoria. Others in the fellowship were Dr Fred Roberts, founder of the Durban Christian Centre, Pastor Tim Salmon, then pastor of the Maritzburg Christian Church, evangelist Nicky van der Westhuizen, of World Mission Evangelism, in Krugersdorp, German evangelist Reinhard Bonnke, of Christ for all Nations and Ray.

Each one of these men came from a different denominational background. Roebert had started off as a traditional Baptist and then moved into the charismatic experience. He eventually cut his links with the Baptist Union of South Africa to start an independent ministry.

Nicky van der Westhuizen had been a prominent evangelist in the Afrikaans-speaking Pentecostal Protestant Church, but had resigned to go it alone in 1978. Van der Westhuizen subsequently dropped out of the leadership after his marriage failed and he sought a divorce and remarried.

Fred Roberts had been a distinguished minister in the Full Gospel Church of God until cutting loose and establishing an independent church in Durban; while Tim Salmon ministered as an independent in Zimbabwe before moving to South Africa.

The German-born Reinhard Bonnke was an officially recognised minister of the Apostolic Faith Mission in South Africa, although his missionary organisation, Christ for all Nations, is international and non-denominational. Bonnke pulled out of South Africa in 1986 and moved his headquarters to Frankfurt, Germany, from where he continues to organise and conduct massive open-air crusades in Africa.

And then there was Ray, with his strong faith and word teaching background, who had burst on the church scene in 1979. These men, despite their strong streak of independence, felt they needed to meet and fellowship together. Each recognised that in some way their ministries were being interwoven and that it would be in the best interests of the kingdom of God, and the nation, if they began to forge some links.

Ed Roebert, who had been praying for a strategy for the nation, was led to contact each one of these men. This led to a meeting of the men and their wives every six weeks, rotating the venue between Durban, Pietermaritzburg, Johannesburg and Pretoria. A strong bond of friendship and commitment grew between them.

It paid handsome dividends on a personal level and on a national basis for the body of Christ. They learnt about each other's doctrinal views and found that some of the stories about their so-called pet doctrines were exaggerated. They found that they had a lot more in common than they had first believed possible. The result of the fellowship has been impressive. Not only did it lead to co-operation between the six men, but it also handsomely benefited evangelist Bonnke, whose ministry prospered considerably from the fellowship.

As the men met over the next three years it became obvious that some type of organisation was required so as to give the many new independent churches, which were starting, better credibility, as well as an official voice in the nation.

It was plain to them that the Lord wanted something positive to flow from their fellowship, which would permeate the whole body of Christ. They developed a high profile within their constituencies, mainly because of the growth and size of their individual churches (except Bonnke, of course, who was totally committed to evangelising in Africa). But besides these men, hundreds of other churches began springing up underneath the umbrella of the fellowships.

Each one of these men (Bonnke on a much smaller scale) had trained hundreds of students who had gone through their churches' Bible schools. Many of these students pioneered independent churches, while maintaining a loose link with their previous 'mother' assembly.

There was a need to maintain unity and to avoid unnecessary competition which sometimes happened when several men arrived in the same small town intent on establishing a church.

Besides the new crop of young student ministers there were also several denominational pastors who had become tired of the restrictions placed on them by the structures of their organisations. They also joined the new spiritual flow.

Although Ray and the other men had no desire to start a new denomination, they were acutely aware that some 'covering' was needed and it was essential that the hundreds of new independent pastors be given official accreditation so as to be able to perform normal pastoral duties, like acting as marriage officers. But they did not want to become top heavy and bound by strict and rigid executive decrees which might stifle the work of God, as sometimes happens within denominational churches.

So they decided to form a loose affiliation of all the independents under the banner of the 'International Fellowship of Christian Churches' (IFCC), which was similar to an association formed in America. The IFCC is not a denomination. Membership is voluntary and the IFCC executive does not interfere in the running of any single church. It acts as a monitor, to ensure proper moral, financial and spiritual conduct is adhered to by those affiliated to the IFCC. Sadly, its code of conduct had to be invoked when one of the founders, Nicky van der Westhuizen, left his wife.

The IFCC was officially launched at a meeting in Durban in August 1985 with over 400 full-time pastors, evangelists and full-time workers attending the meeting. About 250 individual ministries initially joined the IFCC, which has continued to grow at an astonishing rate. By the end of 1991 it had a membership of close to 600 churches and evangelistic ministries, representing over 500,000 Christians throughout the country.

One of the first targets the IFCC set itself was to gain representation as chaplains in the armed forces and to get airtime on the SABC (radio and television). With its membership it could now make claims for legitimate recognition.

Another benefit of the pastors' fellowship was to bring the needs of Reinhard Bonnke's Christ for all Nations organisation into sharp focus. As a result the other members of the fellowship began to channel large amounts of finance into his plan to evangelise Africa 'from Cape Town to Cairo'.

It brought Ray and Reinhard Bonnke into a much closer relationship, which developed into more than just a mutual admiration. They have become deep and sincere friends, with Ray demonstrating this friendship in the most tangible ways by helping to raise tens of thousands of US dollars for Reinhard from friends in America.

The McCauley-Bonnke connection has resulted in the evangelist taking part in several major seminars and conventions staged by Rhema. It was Reinhard who dedicated the land on which the Rhema church is built.

As Reinhard's ministry has expanded, so Ray's connection with him has become even stronger. Besides ministering at Reinhard's first FIRE Conference held in Harare, Zimbabwe, in April 1986, he also shared the platform with him in August of the same year when Reinhard organised a convention in Munich, West Germany. Subsequently he has been invited to be a main speaker at the EuroFire conferences held in Frankfurt in 1987, Birmingham in 1988, and Lisbon in 1990. He has also shared in crusades in Czechoslovakia and in Zaire.

Although some of the original leadership has either left or dropped out, the IFCC is now an established movement in South Africa with Ray the de facto leader and spokesman for its over half a million followers. The IFCC membership consists mostly of independent churches and, although it allows associate membership to denominational individuals, it has no direct influence on the Pentecostal denominations.

One organisation which existed for many years was

the Fellowship of Pentecostal Churches of South Africa. This was an organisation which brought together, on a quarterly basis, leaders of the major Pentecostal denominations in South Africa. It was formed to cement relationships between the denominations, to promote the Pentecostal cause, to share in joint ventures and to display a united front on issues in the country.

These ideals did not quite materialise, although the Fellowship did foster some useful relationships and better understanding among some of the Pentecostal churches. However, to be truthful, the Fellowship did not, especially in the past four or five years, serve any useful purpose in the rapidly changing scene in the country.

Rhema, after being regarded as something akin to a leper in the early founding days of the church, was eventually invited to join the Fellowship and faithfully paid its annual subscriptions and attended meetings regularly. One of Rhema's pastors, Mark Hodgetts, a product of a classical Pentecostal Bible School, who 'defected' to Rhema, became the church's chief delegate on the Fellowship, which was seldom attended by Ray at the beginning.

But as Ray's stature in church circles began to burgeon, he took more interest in the Fellowship and got elected as Vice-chairman of the organisation. Ray's feeling in allowing himself to be elected was that it would improve his effectiveness and give him more credibility among church leaders. Being a man of bold action Ray was not shy in using what muscle the Fellowship had when it came to making a media statement. A situation arose in 1988 when Professor Johan Heyns was moderator of the Dutch Reformed Church.

The Dutch Reformed Church was making some critical steps towards liberalising its racial policy, and

Professor Heyns was in the vanguard and under extreme duress from staunch apartheid supporters among the clergy and from congregations. It was obvious that Professor Heyns' bold leadership was cracking the foundations of the Dutch Reformed Church and that a split was on the way. The division did materialise, causing many heartfelt hurts.

It was against this setting that Ray decided it would be a good Christian deed to rally round the Professor and his leadership, and commend them for their desire to break out of the apartheid tradition. At this time I was given the task of co-ordinating a snap meeting of the Pentecostal Fellowship's top brass with the Dutch Reformed leadership at their headquarters in Pretoria. I was also detailed to prepare a press statement. Before I could release the statement, though, I had to contact the various leaders of the Pentecostal denominations to get their approval and inclusion of their names in the press statement.

It proved a frustrating operation. Having got used to working closely with Ray on all his press releases, which took only minutes to approve and then distribute, I found myself bumping headlong into church bureaucracy. Chief executives either were not available or would have to refer the statement to fellow members before agreeing to be associated with the statement.

Ray and I now began to realise why the Pentecostal Fellowship had failed in its efforts to be a voice in the nation. Its members were totally out of step with modern media communications.

I continued to badger the leaders and read the statement over the phone to all of them, pressurising them to give the press release their approval. The contents of the statement were, in fact, fairly general, with the main point that the Pentecostal churches wanted to express their solidarity with the Dutch Reformed Church in its move away from apartheid in the church.

Having eventually obtained agreement, we sent the statement out to the media. The Pentecostal delegation—which included Ray, Dr F. J. Moller of the Apostolic Faith Mission, Pastor 'Poen' Badenhorst of the Full Gospel Church of God, Pastor Ed Roebert of the IFCC, and myself—met with Professor Heyns and his executive in Pretoria.

Wide media coverage was given to this token of Christian charity and gave the Pentecostals considerable respectability for having got involved in a national issue. There was an unfortunate backlash at a meeting of the Fellowship some months later, however, when the leader of one of the denominations gave notice that he was withdrawing his organisation from the Fellowship because he had not been properly consulted about the press statement on the Dutch Reformed Church. I had personally telephoned the leader in Cape Town and read him the statement. I now found his reason for pulling out more than strange. Some two years after this incident I happened to share a commercial flight with this same leader and realised then that the man had a personal grievance against Ray and had used the press statement as a smokescreen to get out of the Fellowship.

This incident, and the meanderings of the Fellowship for the next two years, made it obvious that the Fellowship was terminally sick and late in 1990 Ray and a few other members began to talk about resuscitating the organisation. Despite the Fellowship's large constituency it was doing nothing to contribute to the changes taking place in the country. It was heavily bound in old-style Pentecostal tradition and sadly lacking in broad representation across the colour line. It seemed, especially at leadership level, to be an almost all-White organisation. So in 1991 Ray, with the full agreement of the executive and the incumbent chairman Dr F. J. Moller, began a process which led to the restructuring of the Fellowship into a stronger and more representative body.

After formally disbanding the old Fellowship, an interim committee then set about forming a new organisation, which is now called the Pentecostal–Charismatic Fellowship of Southern Africa. It was agreed to broaden the title to include a segment of the church, which although Pentecostal in belief, preferred to be known as charismatics, having been birthed out of historical denominations in the Seventies.

When the first official elections took place Ray was voted in as President, and the new executive also included leaders other than Whites. I found myself riding on Ray's coat-tails and was voted in as secretary of the new organisation.

The first thing Ray decided to do was issue a media statement, which I drew up and distributed to newspapers and the television. The main news bulletin on the national TV carried a report on the formation of the new organisation, and the newspapers carried the story prominently the following morning. Unfortunately, some of the newspaper headlines erroneously billed the new organisation as a Rhema creation and caused a ripple of displeasure among some of the Fellowship's membership. One denomination objected quite strongly to the press release, claiming that it was a bit premature and that they needed an assurance that Ray would not make any future media statements without first getting the nod from fellow executive members.

In order to maintain the unity of the organisation, Ray offered an apology and agreed that he would consult with his executive, which he had done anyway with the statement which launched the new organisation.

It was, however, an example of some of the pettiness which still exists within the Pentecostal denominations, who still find it difficult to reconcile the success of Rhema and the prominence that Ray is achieving in the nation. It was, perhaps, more galling for some to see Ray, a non-classical Pentecostal, as the national spokesman for the movement in South Africa!

Despite these minor irritations the restructured organisation has the potential to be a significant platform for Christians to make their will known as the future of South Africa is being shaped. For probably the first time in its history a large portion of Pentecostal believers in South Africa are in a position to talk to one another and to work together on joint projects. More importantly, though, the Fellowship will need to be on its toes to act when it sees any prejudicial moves made against Christians in the formulating of the country's new constitution.

Although Ray has taken a backseat in recent years on moral issues, such as promiscuity, homosexuality and abortion, he has not failed to notice the growing liberalisation of moral attitudes in the country. Pornographic magazines, including imports from America, are proliferating despite efforts to censor them, and homosexuals and lesbians have twice staged 'Gay Liberation' marches in Johannesburg. Divorce is rampant in the country, shocking cases of child abuse are being uncovered daily, while the deadly AIDS virus haunts the medical services of the country who predict thousands of victims dying from 1995 onwards.

These social issues are very real in South Africa today because there has been a steady decline in the moral standards of the country over the past four to five years. They have not gone unnoticed, but the political upheaval and the ongoing unrest tend to overshadow these moral issues. The constant cry in the country has been for freedom, justice and democracy—all very noble thoughts, but far from being achieved while the bitter fighting continues between the political factions.

Thus the focus of most people, including the clergy, has been on these larger-than-life socio-political issues.

One attempt to provide freedom and justice for all in South Africa has been the drafting of a Bill of Rights. Under the Nationalist Party Government there was no Bill of Rights. Now all political groups are clamouring for such a Bill and, in general, it has been welcomed by all South Africans.

Pentecostal Christians, however, have a check about a Bill of Rights and where it could lead to. Although basically in agreement, Ray sees the warning lights flashing when minority groups begin to abuse a Bill of Rights to promote issues which could be anti-Christian. So despite being so closely involved in 1991 with the major political players in South Africa, Ray has in no way deserted his conservative, biblical outlook on personal and public morality.

For this reason the Pentecostal–Charismatic Fellowship is, indeed, an important vehicle for Bible-believing Christians, because it could, with a following of over three million, give an exceptionally strong signal to the authorities (whoever they may be in the future South Africa) that certain moral values cannot be traded in for promiscuous, liberal lifestyles.

The proposed Bill of Rights, naturally, gives protection to religion, but even in this fundamental right, the Christians could face a new challenge.

South Africa has always regarded itself as a Christian Protestant nation, and this is borne out by recent national census figures which put the number of people who regard themselves as Christian as 75 per cent of the thirty-five-million population. Of course, this figure represents millions of people who consider themselves Christian on the basis that their parents may have attended church and that they may have been christened as infants. Nevertheless, a large proportion of these people do, to a lesser or larger degree, hold to Christian values.

Any attempt at extrapolating the figures of genuine, practising Christians would be extremely hazardous, but I would guess it could be as high as 45 per cent of the total population, placing Black Christians far in ascendancy, in numbers, over their White brethren.

The question which immediately follows is: just how many practising Christians hold to the Pentecostal belief? Although one has foundational statistics from the organised Pentecostal denominations, and from Rhema and the IFCC, there are literally thousands of independent Black Pentecostal churches scattered throughout the country. However, daring a speculative guess, I would put the Pentecostal believers at about ten million.

Therefore, the Pentecostal–Charismatic Fellowship of Southern Africa, although claiming only to represent three million people, potentially could more than triple its constituency. Even if it could not succeed in doing this officially, simply because of the vast logistic difficulties in tracking down all the Pentecostal churches, it could nevertheless rely on the sympathy of a multitude of fellow Pentecostal Christians.

The Pentecostal constituency about which I have speculated is hardly recognised by the media or, for that matter, by politicians. This potential muscle has probably never been realised by the Pentecostals either! This vast, mostly silent, Christian constituency could, if mustered, play a significant part in the shaping of the new South Africa.

Ray has seen some of this potential, which is why he was so keen on revamping the old Pentecostal Fellowship and of getting in new blood and, just as important, less White domination.

Pentecostal Christians are slowly beginning to realise that they do carry some clout, especially if it concerns buying power. In 1991 some Christians made a strong protest to a major food store chain about the displaying of girlie magazines on shelves at the checkout points. The managing director, when confronted with the challenge 'either remove the offending magazines or face a boycott of your stores', acted speedily in discontinuing them. Similar complaints have been registered by Pentecostal groups against stores that kept toys glorifying the occult and here, too, the stores have dealt positively with the objections.

So it is becoming apparent that Pentecostals can be not only heard, but have their objections acted upon as well. The question, now, is whether the new Pentecostal–Charismatic Fellowship can mobilise its potential not only to maintain Christian values within society, but use its muscle to promote peace and reconciliation in the nation. With Ray at its head it could possibly play a prominent part in bringing harmony to South Africa over the next few years.

IO

Breaking Barriers

For over four years I had tried to set up a meeting for Ray with Dr Frank Chikane, the charismatic General Secretary of the South African Council of Churches.

Chikane, in addition to Bishop Desmond Tutu, became in the late eighties one of the most powerful churchmen in the country. He was one of the few Black voices that the South African Government could not stifle. The SACC, and men like Bishop Tutu and Chikane, were regarded by many White evangelical Christians as 'radicals', failing to grasp that because of the draconian security laws imposed few Black people really had a voice in the land. The SACC, rightly or wrongly, became an unofficial vehicle for the Black majority, which included the then exiled ANC.

Round about 1987 I gave Ray an audio cassette of a testimony by Chikane. After listening to it, he asked me to try and set up a meeting, because he felt it important to try and bridge the gaps that existed between the various church groupings. It was a radical decision, considering that few of Ray's fellow IFCC pastors would fully understand such contact with the SACC, which was looked upon as a bunch of political activists.

But Ray was prepared to take the risk, because he felt it important to meet Chikane, especially as the maverick Chikane did have a Pentecostal background. Chikane, in fact, is a member of the Apostolic Faith Mission, the largest Pentecostal denomination in South Africa. His church at one time denounced him because of his so-called political activities, but later on restored him, with a full apology, to his former status.

The audio cassette I gave to Ray contained a story of how Chikane had been harassed and beaten by security police, some of whom were reputed to be members of his own church. Yet despite his anguish and suffering Chikane displayed no hatred or bitterness in his testimony, which impressed Ray to seek a meeting with him.

Setting up such a meeting was not easy. The historical churches and the Pentecostals have walked separate roads for many years. Now here was Ray McCauley, of Rhema, making overtures to the SACC. In hindsight one can appreciate why there was so much suspicion at the time and a reluctance to get the two men together.

It took almost four years before Ray and Chikane shook hands and sat down next to each other and discussed church affairs. Every attempt to get them together had met with failure. A private luncheon, arranged at the Rhema Church, was cancelled an hour before because Chikane was called out to an emergency meeting. In fact, as time went by Ray almost despaired of ever meeting with Chikane. In the meantime, though, we had made some inroads through another way when Ray struck up a good relationship with Lutheran

Bishop Manus Buthelezi, who was the President of the SACC.

Bishop Buthelezi had come to a few special Rhema functions and Ray had made a point of meeting and greeting him. Then, when Ray decided to have a private dinner at his home, Bishop Buthelezi and his wife were included in among the guests.

On another occasion Ray visited the Bishop's Lutheran church in Soweto and spoke to some of the staff, and Dick Khoza, one of Rhema's pastors, held a series of Bible studies at the Lutheran church. The desire to meet with Chikane had been echoed to Bishop Buthelezi, but it was Dick Khoza who eventually put together the meeting after he had met with some of the SACC people in Soweto.

The long-awaited meeting took place in an SACC boardroom in their offices in Johannesburg. Chikane's open and friendly reception soon made the Rhema party feel at home, and he and Ray exchanged views on the latest developments in the nation. As they sat there that morning neither realised that he would shortly be clashing in a war of words in the media, or that they would be serving together on a committee that would put together probably the most historic church conference ever held in the country.

Ray left the meeting contented that he had at last made contact and that there was an open door now. During their conversation there had even been mention of Rhema having observer status at the SACC, which possibly might lead to membership of the organisation. Such contemplation is regarded as heresy in a few Right-Wing church organisations. But such is the new openness and eagerness of people to come together in South Africa that seemingly insurmountable barriers are crumbling.

At about the same time as the Chikane meeting Ray

was involved with Dr Louw Alberts, Professor Johan Heyns and other church leaders in putting together a conference for July 1990. The conference had germinated out of an appeal by President F. W. de Klerk in his Christmas message for churches to come forward with proposals for the shaping of the new post-apartheid South Africa.

Because of a newfound awareness of the importance of socio-political affairs, the Pentecostal—evangelical churches had responded positively to such a conference. The historical churches, although agreeing for the need for such a conference, were upset that the event had been initiated by the State President. They felt, rightly, that the church had to remain independent of the State. The result was that the July Conference was placed in jeopardy and it looked like efforts to bring the whole church family together would prove futile.

Ray was included in the original planning committee and a last-ditch attempt to save the conference resulted in a special meeting being held at the SACC offices in June. After lunch together the two groups went into separate caucus meetings before thrashing out the issues on the open floor. Dr Louw Alberts, a devout Christian and a retired member of the South African Atomic Energy Board and adviser to the Government, took the chair for the closed-door session with the evangelical group.

Besides Dr Alberts, there was Ray, the Revd Michael Cassidy, internationally known author and evangelist, Dennis House, an executive of Youth for Christ, and Professor Heyns of the Dutch Reformed Church. I was there as an aide to Ray.

The issues at stake were quite clear: the SACC churches wanted the date changed, the working committee revamped, a new agenda and no involvement by the State. The problem for Dr Alberts' group was the fact that a date, venue and invitations to churches were already organised. To complicate matters further, President de Klerk had shifted appointments to accept an invitation to speak at the July conference.

When Dr Alberts and his group went into the main meeting I honestly didn't see much hope for a compromise. As the meeting unfolded it got worse. On one side of the room sat our group, surrounded by twenty-one delegates, representing the majority of the major denominations in the country. During the earlier parrying I detected a slight degree of contempt for our grouping. It had to be understood though in the context of the role of the churches in the South African political milieu. We were a group who had most of the time sat on the sidelines and criticised the SACC, and now we were attempting to call the shots.

When things got tough the meeting stopped to pray and it was after this that a solution suddenly began to emerge. There was consensus on the need for a conference.

Bishop Manus Buthelezi described the meeting taking place at that moment as 'historic', while Dr Alan Boesak pleaded for the 'utter necessity' of a conference. Dr Boesak, who unfortunately had to stand down a few months later because of marital problems, came out strongly for rescuing the situation. He was sitting opposite Ray, and although the two men had only met briefly on previous occasions, they had struck a common chord and a level of mutual admiration.

Dr Boesak left his chair and came across to whisper something to Ray. After convincing pleas by Ray, Michael Cassidy and some others the meeting galloped to an abrupt and surprising conclusion. All the obstacles melted and decisions, maybe not all that democratic, were made. Most important was the fact that a National Church Conference, lasting five days, was agreed upon for the first week in November 1990.

Chikane commented afterwards: 'A significant thing is happening to the Church in South Africa.' Indeed it was. Never in the history of the country would a conference bring together such a broad spectrum of the church and no one could deny that it came at a critical point in the history of the nation. Despite its sins and failures of the past, it seems obvious to even a casual onlooker that there was a distinct divine flavour about the event. It came when there was a desperate need for peaceful solutions to be offered to the nation.

In the run-up to the November conference it was agreed that the evangelical–Pentecostal group could go ahead with its two-day event in Pretoria. It was projected as a training ground for these church leaders to refine themselves for the major conference later on.

As the steering committee met to prepare the programme and plan the November conference, it became even more apparent how significant the event was regarded overseas. Many international enquiries were received to attend, including requests from the World Council of Churches, the British Council of Churches and other major world church alliances.

The theme of the conference tried to encapsulate the mood of the moment. It was 'Towards a United Christian Witness in a Changing South Africa'. The nation and more so the politicians would watch with great interest for what would emerge from the conference. Despite the diversity of church backgrounds the planning of the conference went ahead with amazing smoothness. The choice of main speakers at the event caused some difficulties, especially when trying to accommodate the charismatic wing of the church. It became patently clear that this part of the body had few academics to offer to speak to the chosen subjects. Recognising Ray's leadership and influence it was decided to give him an 'inspirational' slot on one evening. Not one to get into deep academic papers, this suited Ray admirably.

With everything now ready, it soon came time for the historic conference to begin.

II

Confession Time

Unintentional as it may have been, the starting date of the five-day-long Rustenburg Conference was November 5, the traditional Guy Fawkes commemoration. It certainly proved to be an explosive event.

The first afternoon and evening sessions were conducted by Bishop Tutu, Michael Cassidy, Methodist Bishop Khoza Mgojo, Dr Frank Chikane and Professor Koos Vorster, a Dutch Reformed theologian. Heavyweights all, I wondered how Ray, normally impatient when forced to listen to long, drawn-out theological papers, would survive a week of continuous addresses, workshops and debates. He tried manfully to attend as much of the conference as possible and fulfil his duties as one of the committee responsible for the conference, but he did miss some of the meetings.

This was partially due to an awful tragedy which happened within the congregation. The parents of Mrs Georgie Braithwaite had come out from New Zealand earlier in the year to visit their daughter. The elderly couple got lost while driving and wandered into the Black township of Soweto. Realising that they were lost they had tried to get directions, but at a stop sign a man had thrust a gun at Mrs Harrison's head and demanded money.

In the few moments of confusion that followed Mrs Phyllis Harrison was shot in the arm and the same bullet ricochetted into her husband, Alfred, killing him. Ray received this news while at the conference, and flew straight back to the church.

Ray returned to the conference, but flew back again later in the week to conduct the funeral. The tragedy was turned into a wonderful testimony of Christian love and forgiveness with both the widow and the dead man's daughter publicly declaring they held no grudge against the gunman and that they had forgiven him.

Meanwhile, at the conference, confession and forgiveness had become the dominant theme. Here too Ray made a significant contribution.

It all began on the Tuesday morning with Professor Willie Jonker, a Dutch Reformed theologian from Stellenbosch University in the Cape. During the course of his presentation he made a confession, which proved to be a watershed event of the conference and sparked a controversy which continues and which threatens the very heart of the Dutch Reformed Church in South Africa.

In his paper Professor Jonker said:

> I confess before you and before the Lord, not only my own sin and guilt, and my personal responsibility for the political, social, economical and structural wrongs that have been done to many of you and the results of which you and our whole country are still suffering from, but vicariously I dare also to do that in the name of the NGK, of which I am a

member, and for the Afrikaans people as a whole. I have the liberty to do just that because the NGK at its latest synod has declared apartheid a sin and confessed its own guilt of negligence in not warning against it and distancing itself from it long ago.

Almost spontaneously Bishop Tutu jumped to his feet to receive the confession and offer forgiveness, and the whole conference delegation rose to its feet in applause, signifying the sense that maybe this was a moment of divine grace, and intervention would permeate through the churches, its congregations and ultimately to the nation.

The media, both local and international, grabbed at this confession, and for the rest of the week it was making headline news. Dr Pieter Potgieter, presiding Moderator of the Dutch Reformed Church, endorsed the statement the next morning, and Bishop Tutu added a confession, too, from his side.

Outside the conference hall the media were given a field day, with Dr Andries Treurnicht, a former theologian and leader of the Conservative Party, rejecting the confession. The immediate past State President P. W. Botha also personally expressed his dissatisfaction to Dr Potgieter.

The main focus of confession and apportioning of sin was on the Dutch Reformed Church and the Afrikaans people in particular, but the smugness of the English-speaking church was soon ruffled when Professor Charles Villa-Vincencio, of the University of Cape Town, uttered a confession.

Although acknowledging the historical witness of the English-speaking church, he noted that their liberal protests against apartheid had not been followed up with any 'significant forms of resistance'. He added, pointedly, that English-speakers had reaped immense economic benefits from apartheid, while expressing only polite indignation towards the system.

It was apparent to all that the conference was fast-becoming a confessional, with all churches and denominations acknowledging their faults. It was also obvious that there was a section of the church which, so far, was stunningly silent on the issue of its association with apartheid—the Pentecostal–charismatic grouping.

Ed Roebert, who pastors the fast-growing Hatfield Christian Church in Pretoria and who shares in the leadership of the IFCC with Ray, broached the possibilities of a Pentecostal-charismatic confession.

Ray readily agreed and I was delegated to muster together the various Pentecostal-charismatic delegates for a hastily convened meeting in a hotel room. Besides the IFCC there were representatives from three major Pentecostal denominations and from a cluster of charismatic churches loosely connected under the name of 'Network Ministries'.

I was charged with drawing up a draft confession which the leaders then debated, and it began to emerge that although personally willing to identify with the document, some were reluctant to take such a dramatic step without consulting further with their executives. This reluctance reflected the dilemma of some of the Pentecostal denominations who are still in the throes of breaking out of apartheid structures. Although the Dutch Reformed Church has taken the main assault for its very intimate involvement with apartheid, the Pentecostal Church, especially those in predominantly Afrikaans-speaking rural areas, carries much of the same guilt and same racial attitude.

As the discussion went on in the hotel room, it became clear that the Pentecostal denominations would not be able to join in any general confession. But the Revd Derek Crumpton, from East London, and a prime mover within the charismatic movement, fully supported the principle, and he assisted me in redrafting the confession which Ray agreed to read out that evening to the conference.

Ray was scheduled to speak on the Wednesday night. I had watched some of the big names in church circles eye Ray with curiosity during the opening sessions of the conference. It was obvious that he had many serious critics, especially among the more traditional church leaders, who could not figure out how Ray could have even been on the committee which had pulled together the conference. So when Ray came to speak in the evening it was easy to pick out some of Rhema's hardest critics. They were there to hear—and maybe pass judgement?

Of course, the audience was not a typical Pentecostal–charismatic one, so the spontaneous 'Amens' and 'Hallelujahs' which punctuate a typical Ray sermon were few and far between. Yet he preached with his usual conviction on the subject of unity, using John 17:20–23 as his text. He soon had the attention of his fellow churchmen.

As he closed his sermon, he read 1 Corinthians 13:4–6 and then began to read out the confession which we had drawn up late that afternoon. The people sitting in the hall did not quite grasp the significance of what Ray was saying, but several of the top theologians sat riveted as Ray concluded the confession with a simple one liner: 'Please forgive us.' (See Appendix A for more details.)

There was no thunderous applause, but rather a polite acceptance of the confession. Unfortunately there were still reservations. Partly, I believe, because there were some sceptics who thought Ray was getting on the band-wagon, and partly because many had been genuinely surprised, thinking that the Pentecostal charismatic church just was not sensitive to the whole socio-political issue in South Africa.

At breakfast the next morning the dining room was buzzing with conversation about the previous evening's confession by Ray, and by lunch time a group of Black evangelicals and Pentecostals met separately with him. This group consisted of Concerned Evangelicals, led by the Revd Caesar Molebatsi from Soweto, and representatives from the Relevant Pentecostal Witness, led by Pastor Japie Lapoorta from Cape Town. Both these organisations had been formed because of their disgust with their White counterparts, who with a few isolated exceptions were content to play along with the apartheid system. As a result these two Black groups had been regarded by some White Pentecostal and evangelical leaders as 'radicals' and of compromising the gospel by getting involved in political affairs.

The leaders of these groups had listened and read carefully copies of the confession which I had made available to the meeting and the media, and they were moved by the sincerity of Ray's words and intentions to become more relevant to the changing situation in the country.

The private meeting led to a determination by those concerned to work out ways and means of restoring broken fellowship and of seeing where we could co-operate in areas of mutual concern. If nothing else was to be achieved from the Rustenburg Conference this at least would be one positive notch of bringing together sections of the Pentecostal/evangelical church in South Africa. But there were many other positive spin-offs from the conference, some of them of benefit to Rhema. A major step was made at the conference with the historic drafting of what is now known as the 'Rustenburg

Declaration', a document to which the majority of churches, to a lesser or larger degree, were able to agree.

Since then the Declaration has come in for considerable criticism from Right-Wing Dutch Reformed leaders, who see the document as a sell-out of Whites and of the beliefs of their race-related dogma.

Criticism of the Declaration also came from fundamentalists, who felt that the document was too political and betrayed the gospel. The fundamentalists, some of whom attended the conference, were appalled to see Ray on such good terms with Bishop Tutu and other liberal churchmen, and perplexed when Ray avoided getting involved with debates on abortion, pornography, Marxism and other typical fundamentalist agendas. For the next several months fundamentalist newsletters carried a tirade of sniping remarks aimed at the Rustenburg Declaration, obliquely taking pot-shots at Ray.

There was a minor backlash among some of the pastors under the IFCC banner, who were concerned that Ray was becoming politicised. Similar concern was echoed from a few congregational members. Some thought Ray was compromising and going soft on the 'big' sins, not realising that the major issue of the Rustenburg Conference had been the matter of the church's complicity in apartheid and that dealing with this issue so openly and frankly had, hopefully, begun a healing process within the wider body of the church in South Africa.

The fundamentalist critics found it difficult to grasp that racism and bigotry were sins just as 'big' as those traditionally flogged from their pulpits. They also failed to comprehend fully that unless the issue of racism and equal justice and political rights for all were not dealt with, then there would be no prosperous future for South

Africa because it would collapse into a Beirut syndrome. Abortion rights and lusts of the flesh would be the least of the church's concerns if a catastrophic civil war were to erupt.

Ray bravely fielded all the criticism, patiently explaining to those who bothered to seek an answer to why he was involved, assuring them that they need not fear that he was leading Rhema or the IFCC into any political quagmire.

There was, of course, a lot of positive comment too, especially from the strong Black contingent within Rhema and the IFCC, who were excited to see Ray taking such a strong leadership role.

Historical church leaders were jolted into a realisation that Ray was sincere about being involved in the socio-political changes which were happening in the country. The Rhema Church and its affiliates in the IFCC could no longer be regarded as simple 'pie-in-the-sky' churches who did not care for the social needs of people during their sojourn on earth.

Early in 1991 the Rustenburg Committee met to review the conference and to discuss the next step forward. It was decided that the Declaration needed to be popularised and disseminated at grassroots level.

The other strategy was to distribute the Rustenburg Declaration to political leaders, including President de Klerk, and then to follow this up with an official deputation of the Rustenburg Committee.

The first meeting to be arranged was with President de Klerk at Tuynhuys, the official residence of heads of State of South Africa, in Cape Town, in the afternoon of March 14, 1991.

I flew with Ray, arriving mid-morning, and assembled with other committee members at a Roman Catholic church near Tuynhuys. There was some discussion over lunch as to issues which might be raised with President de Klerk. There was some dissension because some delegates were keen to introduce the matter of a public debate on the plight of political refugees and the assistance of the United Nations High Commission on Refugees. The matter was eventually shelved and the delegates then strolled over to the historical Tuynhuys.

The meeting was scheduled to begin at three and it was expected to finish soon after four, as the President had to prepare for a formal dinner party later that evening. As it turned out, however, the President and the Rustenburg committee members became so involved in their discussion that it was well after five o'clock before Louw Alberts and Frank Chikane led the smiling group out of the room and outside to meet with a barrage of media people who had patiently waited for over two hours.

During the discussion of the Declaration the President had made the point that he felt the churchmen had gone a bit too far on some issues and had begun to dabble in the political realm. He made a strong plea to the churchmen to keep within their parameters and that politicians, in turn, should keep within their boundaries.

The matter of whether the Nationalist Government should repent and confess for the errors of apartheid was touched on at the Tuynhuys meeting, and was to emerge later on as a major point of debate within the Dutch Reformed Church family.

Although President de Klerk and the Government were willing to concede that the ideology of apartheid had brought suffering and shame, they still defended the past, claiming, in essence, that it was all right for that period of time. That generation had not seen it as evil or wrong, but now the present generation were more enlightened.

This rather hazy argument says, in fact, that apartheid

was right in the past, but now it is wrong. For the average person in the street the matter may not appear to be an issue, but within the Afrikaner family and the Dutch Reformed Church it is a serious matter of contention. If apartheid is totally and unequivocally renounced as political and doctrinal error by the Dutch Reformed Church, then it means that every minister in the church who supported apartheid taught heresy and that every congregation was taught error. By implication it seriously questions the credibility of all Dutch Reformed ministers and their ability to handle the Bible fairly and justly.

The fact is that many Afrikaners have seen the truth and many Dutch Reformed ministers have stepped into the light, but many are still hiding behind the convoluted argument that apartheid was right for a certain time in history, but is now wrong.

Although many Afrikaners may say that the political ideology of apartheid is now wrong, they may very well still harbour racist beliefs in their hearts.

This sombre thought gains considerable credibility when looking at the Right-Wing political groups who, by and large, are all staunch members of a break-away 'Whites-only' Dutch Reformed Church. But as Ray and many others have said and preached, the abolition of all racists laws will not, in itself, change the heart attitude of people.

Racism was systematically and practically implemented in South Africa over a period of forty years. Its breeding ground was not only among the Afrikaner— the British colonial rule also injected their paternalistic attitude towards people of other skin-colours. The combination produced the most race-conscious country in the world.

In his crusade to bring reconciliation, Ray has realised that a simple born-again experience is not necessarily

going to change racial attitudes. His study of the Bible
has led him to an understanding of the need to break
with the traditions of the past—and one very strong
family tradition in South Africa, passed down from
father to son, is that White Afrikaners are a superior
people.

He has had to deal with this attitude even within the
Rhema congregation, and when challenged by the word
of God some have opted to go their own way and leave.
Many more, however, have thankfully come to a
realisation of their false beliefs and into a new freedom
of the gospel. Ray fervently believes the cliché that the
Christians need to be part of the solution and not part
of the problem and so begin the job of restoration and
reconciliation in South Africa.

Although South Africa is webbed with violence, anger,
bitterness and suspicion, there is a huge reservoir of
goodwill. Ray had a first-hand encounter of this when
the Rustenburg committee, following on from the
meeting with Mr de Klerk, next went to see Nelson
Mandela.

The meeting took place on April 17, 1991 at the ANC
offices in downtown Johannesburg. Besides Mr Mandela
the ANC delegation included top executive members,
among them some who were also reported to hold
membership with the South African Communist Party.

The church delegation seemed to be overwhelmed by
the occasion. The statesmanlike bearing of Mr Mandela
seemed to mesmerise the Rustenburg committee, who
were softly rebuked by the ANC leader when he pointed
out that the meeting needed to start with a prayer!

Mr Mandela held the centre stage for most of the
meeting and fascinated Ray and the delegation with a
glimpse of his life in prison on the Robben Island. He
spoke of how his Christian belief had sustained him, and

of how visits by a Dutch Reformed prisons chaplain had encouraged him, especially when he had been ill. He sadly recounted how the prison authorities had removed the chaplain when they believed he was getting too friendly.

A question which still bothers many White South Africans is the alliance of the ANC with the South African Communist Party, and this issue was raised with Mr Mandela.

He was forthright in his response. The alliance, for the present time, had a common enemy, the Nationalist Party Government, and until they had vanquished the apartheid Government the Alliance would continue. He gave the assurance, however, that once the goal of a truly democratic society had been achieved, the ANC would part company with the Communist Party.

Although this is the stated view of the ANC, many Christian fundamentalists and Right-Wing political extremists do not believe this will ever happen. There is continued conjecture about 'hidden agendas', and one scenario, floated by the Right Wing, is that the ANC is under the control of the Communists now and is using them as a front, and only when political power is achieved will this be disclosed.

It has been interesting to note that two of the most prominent churchmen in the anti-apartheid struggle, Bishop Tutu and Alan Boesak, both made sharp criticism of Communism in 1991, with the Bishop emphasising that it was impossible for a person to hold the Marxist ideology and still be a Christian. Mr Boesak, who stepped down from his church during 1991 following his divorce, echoed similar thoughts. However, his reservations about the Alliance did not stop him from joining the ANC and accepting a leadership position in the Western Cape.

Ray visited Hungary in 1990 and Czechoslovakia in 1991, and has a pragmatic outlook on Communism and therefore accepted Mr Mandela's explanation with the sincerity with which it was given. Marxist ideologies have not only crumbled in Eastern Europe, but neighbouring African territories like Mozambique and Angola have also rejected Communism.

Mr Mandela further impressed the church delegation with his warm and genuine respect for the clergy. He explained that Black people had a high regard for the church, because often it was through the work of missionaries and other church institutions that many Black leaders had received a good education. He firmly stressed that the ANC is committed to freedom of religious expression, and by the time the meeting drew to a close Mr Mandela had won a place in the hearts of most of the Rustenburg committee.

As the meeting was breaking up I hustled Ray to get next to Mr Mandela so that I could snap a picture of the two men together. While they chatted briefly Ray took the opportunity to apologise for any wrong impression he may have gained from the 'Are you a Christian?' controversy which Ray had sparked the previous year.

Mr Mandela turned to Ray and nodded while he said: 'Let's leave the past where it belongs.'

Ray returned home that evening truly impressed by the warmth and sincerity of Mr Mandela, amazed at his humility and gentle spirit. Ray could detect no bitterness or animosity, despite the years of deprivation in a prison cell. Although he may not have demonstrated a charismatic brand of Christianity, he certainly bore the marks of Christian charity and forgiveness.

For the rest of the year the Rustenburg Committee made contact with other major political groups to discuss

Frank Chicane (front left), Nelson Mandela, Ray, and Professor Heyns (right) at a meeting of the Rustenburg Committee

the Declaration. However, there was one important political party which refused outright. The Rustenburg committee felt strongly that they needed to meet with Dr Andries Treurnicht, leader of the Conservative Party. But all their overtures were rejected. The closing of the Afrikaner ranks with demands for partition and threats of civil war remain a constant flashpoint in the transition which South Africa is experiencing.

The seriousness of the Right-Wing threats were demonstrated in August 1991 when State President F. W. de Klerk was scheduled to speak at the town hall in the farming town of Ventersdorp.

President de Klerk flew in by helicopter to find the town hall ringed with militant Right Wingers armed with guns, shields, and batons. Armed policemen and police dogs faced the baying mob. Violence erupted when Whites began to stone a passing taxi which contained Blacks.

In the ensuing battle three people were killed and dozens injured in a night that saw Afrikaner pitted against Afrikaner. It was an ugly event, touching the very soul of the Afrikaner people in South Africa.

On the Sunday that followed what the media termed the 'Battle of Ventersdorp', the ex-minister of Law and Order, Mr Adriaan Vlok, attended a morning service at Rhema. Mr Vlok had met Ray some years previously at an amateur wrestling tournament, and had indicated that he would like to visit Rhema some day. When he confirmed early in 1991 that he would like to come to a service in August, the visit was duly noted on the Rhema calendar.

Then, when the date drew near, Ray wondered whether it was such a good idea to have Minister Vlok attend a service. Mr Vlok, a professing Christian, held one of the most controversial cabinet posts. As Minister of Law and Order he was in charge of the police and security forces, and as the explosive spiral of violence continued in the country it was Mr Vlok's office which caught all the flak. The police were continually being accused of bias and of promoting violence in certain instances. Allegations of 'hit squads' and other rumours abounded, and there were calls for Mr Vlok to resign his cabinet post. The Minister of Defence, General Magnus Malan, found himself under similar pressure to quit.

So with all the controversy surrounding Mr Vlok, Ray and some of the Rhema Board members had second thoughts about the wisdom of his being seen in Rhema. Some discreet enquiries were made to find out whether he was still keen to attend, with the hope that maybe he would like to cancel. But the reply came back: he was keenly looking forward to attending the service!

Ray consulted some of the Rhema pastors, and it was agreed that Mr Vlok and his wife should be made welcome and that he was, in fact, attending in his personal capacity and not as a Government representative.

Ray's chief concern had been for the many Black supporters of Rhema who lived in areas where violence and fighting had taken place and where alleged police involvement had been seen. He did not want Black members of the congregation to feel offended, recognising that the old style 'White thinking' was a thing of the past. Decisions in the new South Africa needed to be made with due consideration of all people, Black and White.

As it turned out Mr Vlok's visit caused no undue ripples within the church, and it seemed that the minister, though unaccustomed to the charismatic praise and worship tradition, thoroughly enjoyed the service, and one could not help seeing a tear on his cheek while communion was being shared.

12

The Quest for Peace

After the euphoria of the release of Nelson Mandela, and the unbanning of the ANC and the South African Communist Party, the lines of the future political battle slowly began to emerge.

For most of 1990 the ANC, despite its unsettling (to Whites mostly) talk about nationalisation, could hardly put a foot wrong. Mr Mandela was the darling of the media, both locally and overseas. He toured nations of the world and was feted almost as a head of state.

In South Africa the ANC postured itself to give the impression that it was the 'government in waiting', and the powerful Zulu grouping of Chief Mangosuthu Buthelezi found itself being shoved into the background by the media and by political commentators.

For several months the ANC juggernaut vaunted its newfound freedom to express itself, and the majority of the South African Black population was caught up in an 'Uhuru' (freedom) frenzy that had once marked the liberation of other African States that had once been British colonies.

However, running parallel with the elation of the unbanning of political parties and leaders, was a growing shadow of violence which threatened to pitch the nation into civil war.

A profound Bible principle is that what you sow you reap, and the sad fact of South Africa is that a lot of bad seed has been sown in the past. The forty-odd years of apartheid were upheld and maintained by an iron-fisted police force backed up by an over-zealous Special Branch which arrested and tortured and became almost a law unto itself.

Like most regimes which grossly afflict basic human rights, more and more brute force was needed to maintain the status quo, and so a culture of violence was birthed. This culture of violence contaminated the whole nation. It spilled over into the ranks of rival Black political groups, notably in the province of Natal where the United Democratic Front (UDF), a surrogate for the ANC (until it was unbanned) began to make political inroads into the once virgin territory of Chief Buthelezi.

Even before the 'normalisation' of February 2, 1990, pitched battles between rival groups had forced the South African Government to declare States of Emergency in many areas and bring in the army to help maintain law and order.

There had been hopes that with the release of Mr Mandela a truce would be forged with Chief Buthelezi, and that brutal attacks and reprisal raids which were killing dozens of people and leaving hundreds homeless each week, would be ended. Whether by deliberate design or poor judgement, the ANC delayed a meeting of Mandela and Buthelezi, although there were some negotiations at a lower level.

The two leaders did eventually meet, but not before many more acts of violence had been committed and relationships between the Zulu Chief and the ANC had deteriorated to zero. Instead of defusing the volatile climate between these rival groups, the wick had sadly been primed for a bloody conflict which racked the conscience of the nation.

On the other side of the political spectrum the White backlash was gathering force under the collective leadership of Dr Andries Treurnicht of the Conservative Party, and Mr Eugene Terreblanche who demanded an all-White independent state. Mr Terreblanche's followers, flouting neo-Nazi symbols and openly brandishing firearms at public meetings, threatened to defend their 'rights', rejecting outright the notion of Black domination.

Complicating the issue of violent political confrontation was the fact that the South Africa police, because of their past history of maintaining the pillars of apartheid, was hardly seen as a neutral, peace-keeping force. The police were accused of favouring the ultra-Right-Wing groups and of being sympathetic towards Chief Buthelezi's Inkatha Freedom Party and of being anti-ANC.

The allegations were given greater credence by a series of newspaper exposés of secret 'Death Squads' within the South African security forces, who were blamed for the 'elimination' of prominent anti-government organisers over the years. Commissions of Enquiry into police action at mass marches and at riots painted a grim picture of questionable operations and sinister intrigue. A haunting 'Third Force' was blamed by the ANC, but efforts by all involved failed to define who or what this 'Force' was.

As the momentous year of 1990 faded away, 1991

arrived with the same agonies of political violence, which seemed to spatter over into everyday life. Bank robberies, muggings, hi-jacking of trucks and private vehicles, rape and murder glared at the South African public in the daily newspaper and television headlines.

Death orgies continued in Natal between Inkatha and ANC members, but more chilling were the bloody outbreaks in and around Johannesburg, including mass-acres on commuter trains when innocent passengers were gunned down and hurled out of windows of speeding coaches.

Funeral processions became targets for anonymous gunmen who ruthlessly mowed down men, women and children. In the chilling hysteria of this blood-letting, reprisal raids were launched in townships by crazed mobs who looted, burned and murdered, not knowing or caring who their victims were.

The curse of violence had become endemic in South Africa.

It was against this agonising backdrop that Ray got involved in what became known as the National Peace Initiative. Certainly he was one of many South Africans who were desperately concerned about the deteriorating situation in the country. Political leaders across the spectrum expressed concern. Community leaders, the general public and the media chorused for concrete steps to stop the violence.

The charges and counter-charges of State involvement in the unrest continued to foment more suspicion and distrust. The far Right-Wing Boere lumped all the blame on the ANC. Inkatha lashed out at the ANC, side-swiping the Government as well. And the ANC targeted the so-called 'Third Force', the police and radical Inkatha supporters.

This extraordinary web of confusion and conspiracy

was brought dramatically to Rhema's attention when a church youth leader in the dingy, strife-torn township of Alexander had an amazing escape from certain death.

A brutal attack with AK 47s left seventeen people dead in the township—the mysterious gunmen fleeing the scene before anyone could call the police. Gabriel Ngwenya, aged twenty, and actively involved as a youth leader for the church, was asked by some of the grieving families to conduct an all-night funeral vigil in one of the homes of the deceased. The vigil, attended by relatives and close friends, was scheduled to last until sunrise.

At about one o'clock in the morning the mourners suddenly heard a commotion in the unlit streets outside, and Gabriel and some relatives went to investigate. They heard shouting, and shots being fired. Neighbours, also aroused by the noise, warned everyone to return to their homes and lock themselves in.

Gabriel and the mourners retreated to the safety of the house to continue their vigil. Suddenly loud thumping and shouts at the front door startled the mourners. Young Gabriel recounts how one of the older men in the house went to the door, armed with a firearm and yelled out that if anyone tried to enter he would shoot. As this confrontation was going on Gabriel remembers looking up and seeing a gunman suddenly appear at a wide window and with methodical accuracy put a bullet through the head of the man at the door.

The front door then burst open and several masked gunmen entered and began shooting indiscriminately at the stunned mourners.

The horror of the moment was graphically recalled in Gabriel's own words:

I was standing behind a woman as the door swung open. I heard screams and the sound of shots. Bullets struck the lady in front of me and she fell backwards, knocking me onto the floor. As I lay on the floor other bodies crashed down on top of me.

The shooting and screaming stopped for a moment. Then an elderly woman in the corner began crying and begging the gunmen to spare her.

I opened my eyes and peeped and saw the gunmen, all wearing balaclavas, pointing their guns and threatening the woman. For some reason they turned away and left her grovelling in the corner.

One of the men came towards where I was lying in a tangle of bodies and blood and pointed the gun at the people sprawled on the floor.

I realised he was going to make sure everyone was dead. I shut my eyes and silently prayed. I heard the bullets thudding into the body on top of me and then a hot pain in my leg as bullets ripped through my flesh. Then the shooting stopped and the killers ran out of the house.

Young Gabriel was later taken to the hospital where his ordeal continued when a group of men tried to find out if anybody had survived the massacre. Quick thinking by the nursing staff, who sensed the men might try to kill Gabriel, kept them from finding the young man. On his release from hospital, and afraid of a possible threat to his life, Gabriel was taken to Rhema's 'Hands of Compassion' farm, for protection and to recuperate.

This chilling episode, multiplied countless times in the lives of thousands of Black South Africans, brought the violence issue starkly to Ray's notice.

Black Rhema congregants repeatedly told stories of death and horror that stalked the townships at night. The violence often seemed remote to Whites, who were safely tucked away in their warm beds in suburbs many miles away from the havoc of the townships.

It became blatantly clear that the church not only

needed to get involved, but that it had to play its role as peacemaker in a nation being ripped further apart.

The call for peace constantly echoed across the country, but somehow everyone seemed paralysed to do anything positive, outside of issuing plaintive appeals for calm through the media.

It was with this heightening tension that Ray asked me to co-ordinate a private dinner party at his home and which, in my opinion, was the seedbed for the involvement of a group of churchmen in the resultant National Peace Initiative.

The dinner, held on Friday, April 19, 1991, was the third of what I dubbed 'VIP dinners'. Ray had conceived of the idea of inviting prominent church or political leaders to a private dinner in an effort to build bridges and to get a better grasp of the fast-changing situation in the country.

Among the guests to dinner on that night were Frank Chikane and his wife, and Professor Johan Heyns and his wife. As the evening proceeded, with Chikane sharing some of his humiliating experiences suffered as a result of apartheid, the conversation embraced the mood of violence in the country.

It was during this informal time at the dinner table that the thought of the church getting involved in the peace process took firm root. The tension between the Government and the ANC was extremely taut at that time because of an 'ultimatum' which had been sent to President de Klerk and published in the newspapers. There was speculation that the exploratory talks that were going on between the two groups could be jeopardised.

This crisis was mentioned at the dinner table, which resulted in some hurried phone calls the following day involving the church leaders, President de Klerk and

Nelson Mandela. The outcome was a cooling of emotions and the immediate confrontation was averted.

Besides this issue the dinner conversation focused, naturally, on the violence in the land. President de Klerk had initiated what was being billed as a 'Conference on Violence and Intimidation' which was to be held in Pretoria on May 24 and 25, 1991.

The concept was to bring all the opposing political parties and other interest groups together so as to tackle the issue of violence head-on. The idea was good, but it proved to be a tactical blunder by President de Klerk. The liberation movements, like the ANC, the PAC and others on the Left Wing, rejected the conference because it had been called by the State President. Their argument was that Government could not act as player and umpire at the same time. There was no neutrality in the process, they argued.

So, although the concept was hailed as a breakthrough, it floundered immediately by failing to get the support of the ANC. Chief Buthelezi and his Inkatha Freedom Party, on the other hand, seized the opportunity to attend the conference. They saw it as a chance to demonstrate their eagerness for peace in contrast to the spoiling tactics of the ANC.

This controversial debate circled the dinner table and there was a general consensus between Chikane, Heyns and Ray that the church needed to step in and play a role in getting all the parties to the conference table.

As we sipped coffee together that evening none of us could have conceived the path that lay ahead and of just how involved Ray would become in the search for peace in South Africa. Long, frustrating hours of meetings, last-minute dashes to airports on shuttle diplomacy awaited him over the next four months.

But before the churchmen's peace initiative was put

into action, efforts were made to try and rescue President de Klerk's Pretoria Peace Summit. Although the ANC were dogmatic on the principle that the Government had no right to call the conference, they were anxious to talk peace.

Chikane, acting as linkman, tried valiantly with some others to patch up the situation, but found the Government just as stubborn. They refused to back down on the calling of the Pretoria Summit and were determined that it would go ahead and that those who failed to attend would have to suffer the consequences. It was a very unhappy affair.

A series of events began to unfold and, without over spiritualising them, it is possible to see with hindsight a distinctly divine flavour.

Following the dinner at Ray's home a hurriedly convened and very informal meeting took place at the South African Council of Churches offices in Johannesburg. Those present were Frank Chikane, Johan Heyns and myself. Dr Louw Alberts, because of his valuable role in the Rustenburg Committee, was also invited, but could not attend. The discussion ranged around the latest attempts to get the ANC into the Pretoria Summit. It became apparent that there was little chance of saving the Summit, so thoughts were turned towards a second peace conference, which would embrace the ANC, the Government and the Inkatha Freedom Party.

It was decided that Chikane would explore the possibilities with the ANC leadership, that Professor Heyns would speak to the President, and that Ray would contact Chief Buthelezi and try to convince him that if the church leaders convened a second conference the Inkatha Freedom Party would get a fair deal.

Driving home from an early morning work-out at a

local gym, Ray felt a sudden urge to make contact with Chief Buthelezi. As he recounted afterwards, 'I felt that it was God's Spirit telling me to go and see the Chief Minister.'

Ray called me on his carphone and asked me to see whether I could arrange a meeting with Chief Buthelezi, saying that we would be prepared to fly to his headquarters at Ulundi, set in the rolling hills of Zululand.

Having made previous appointments with Ulundi and knowing what a hectic schedule Chief Buthelezi had, I honestly doubted my chances of getting a meeting at such short notice. However, I contacted a former newspaper colleague of mine, Suzanne Vos, who is a senior member of the Inkatha Freedom Party and their chief media spokesperson. I asked her on the phone to see whether she could influence the Chief's timetable, while I sent a fax request to the Ulundi office.

To my amazement everything clicked into place and we were given an appointment. A twin-engined plane was chartered and Ray, Dick Khoza, a Rhema pastor, Gordon Calmeyer, Rhema's Missions Director, and I took off from Lanseria Airport on a sunny Thursday morning, banking steeply to head eastwards to Ulundi, about ninety minutes' flying time away.

It was now May 16, with the Pretoria Peace Summit only eight days away. Ray's main purpose in wanting to see Chief Buthelezi was to sound out the possibility of a second peace conference. By now it had been accepted that the ANC and other Left-Wing organisations would not be attending the Pretoria Summit, and the news media had begun speculating on a follow-up conference.

The reaction, initially, to a second or follow-on conference had not been too positive from either the

Government or the Inkatha Freedom Party. The Government's concern was that it did not want to lose face or make any commitments in view of the fact that the first conference had not yet taken place. The Zulu leader was sceptical and suspicious about who would convene any second conference. This was the basic reason for Ray's visit to Ulundi.

Years before—in 1987—Ray and three Rhema colleagues had flown to Ulundi to visit and make personal contact with Chief Buthelezi. I had helped to organise that meeting and had been in the group that had visited the Chief. Ray's purpose on that occasion had been pure and simple. He had often heard about Chief Buthelezi's Christian commitment and desired to meet him on a first-hand basis and to pray with him, recognising that as a leader of considerable importance he had a role to play in any future developments of the country.

Our meeting on that morning in 1987 had begun on a very cautious note and we had sat rather stiffly around a large oak boardroom table with Chief Buthelezi smiling benignly at us and peering at Ray over the rims of his spectacles. Ray had made a short speech saying how much we appreciated his dedication to assist peaceful change in South Africa and how Christians were praying for him. He had then presented him with a Bible.

Chief Buthelezi gracefully accepted the accolades and the gift, and then seemed to pause, waiting for the real agenda. There was none, and the Chief became quite emotional when he realised that Ray had been prepared to fly all that way just to express his Christian love and to pray with him. From that moment the meeting became more informal and relaxed, and we finished up being invited to lunch and spending almost four hours with the Chief instead of the designated one hour that had been booked for us.

Ray with Chief Buthelezi in Ulundi

From that first meeting Ray had invited the Chief to attend Rhema any time he was in Johannesburg, and had invited him to a private dinner party. Due to unforeseen circumstances the Chief never took up any of these invitations. However the occasional letters and faxes of encouragement from Ray's desk maintain an important link. It was because of this link, forged I believe on their mutual Christian faith, that gave Ray the open door to fly down and have a crucial meeting with Chief Buthelezi and to gather valuable background knowledge which would help during the protracted peace initiative just around the corner.

As the light aircraft threaded its way gingerly through the mountains which guarded the Ulundi airstrip, Ray fidgeted with his seatbelt as he contemplated his approach to Chief Buthelezi. Ray was firmly convinced that it was the Lord who had urged this meeting, but he was not too sure what the strategy would be. In broad terms he genuinely wanted to meet Buthelezi and encourage him spiritually, and secondly to discuss the problem of the violence in view of the impending Summit.

We were met at the airport by a KwaZulu government vehicle and driven the twelve-odd kilometres to the impressive Legislative Assembly buildings. Once we'd completed the security formalities we were escorted up some stairs and along several passages through security doors from where we spilled into a neatly furnished reception room. A few moments' wait and then the bespectacled, smiling face of Chief Buthelezi appeared and ushered us into a committee room.

Chief Buthelezi sat at the focal point of the dark-wooded circular table with two aides on his left, and on his right Ray, myself, Gordon Calmeyer and colleague Dick Khoza, who as a member of a minor African tribe was finding his visit quite inspiring, being so close to the seat of power of the famous Zulu nation.

Around the walls of the circular room were a hundred or more photographs of Buthelezi with international heads of state, politicians and other famous dignitaries whom he had met. At a quick glance it looked like a kaleidoscope of a giant page of history unfurled against the wall.

After the usual small talk Ray edged onto the subject of violence which allowed Buthelezi to express his deep-seated concern and frustration at the events which were tearing the country apart. He strongly rejected the media perception and propaganda drumbeat which tried to lay most of the blame on his Inkatha supporters. He disclosed details of negotiations which he had with the ANC as well as a very private meeting with Nelson Mandela in a hotel room in Durban.

Ray then shifted the discussion towards the Pretoria peace conference and broached the concept of church involvement in trying to facilitate or mediate in the issues which were keeping the political parties from serious negotiations. At this point Ray made mention of the now famous Rustenburg Committee and its possible role in facilitating peace in the country.

This met with a sharp and sudden change in mood and an unbridled show of anger, which caught us off guard. As Buthelezi composed himself and calmed down, his thrust was clearly against certain people who served on the Rustenburg Committee, mainly Bishop Desmond Tutu and the South African Council of Churches General Secretary Frank Chikane. Most of the hostility, though, was poured out on former Nobel Peace Prize winner Bishop Tutu.

Although we were aware that there was some ill-feeling between Buthelezi and Tutu, which we had gathered from our visit in 1987, we were a little taken aback by the depth of the bitterness which seemed to exist.

Over the years Buthelezi followed a pacifist line in his struggle against apartheid, in contrast to the outright terror tactics of the ANC who chose to fight an underground war against the South African Government. Buthelezi also opposed the international sanctions which injured the national economy and forced tens of thousands of people out of work.

The use of sanctions, argued Buthelezi, was only hurting Blacks and it was on this issue and various others that the Zulu chief clashed with Bishop Tutu, who was perceived to be backing the ANC liberation efforts and snubbing the Zulu leader.

This was exacerbated by the fact that Chief Buthelezi is a devoted member of the Anglican Church and felt that the head of his church, Bishop Tutu, even if they disagreed on political strategies, should have given him more pastoral care and encouragement, instead of, as he perceived it, aligning himself with the ANC against the Chief.

After listening for some while and enjoying a brief interlude for coffee and sandwiches, Ray tried to explain that the Rustenburg Committee was not merely a front for the South African Council of Churches, but genuinely represented the broadest possible spectrum of the church in the country.

Ray broached the possibility of a second peace conference, with the church, in the form of the Rustenburg Committee, acting as the convener.

There was resistance to the idea at first, because Buthelezi took the line that the ANC and the other liberation organisations should attend the Pretoria Summit because of the seriousness of the situation in the country. But as the discussion went on, it became apparent that he was not dogmatically tied to that position and, in fact, was ready to concede that a further conference would have to be called if any progress was to be made in the search for peace.

Ray, sensing this concession, pressed the Rustenburg Committee idea a bit harder and it seemed at one stage that Buthelezi was acceding to the concept.

Having had some sandwiches with our mid-morning tea and coffee we had thought we would leave immediately after our appointment, but Chief Buthelezi extended his hospitality to us to join him and members of his cabinet for lunch. Also joining us was the New Zealand High Commissioner to Zimbabwe, who had flown in from Harare to see the Chief.

The luncheon provided some interesting interaction from some of the cabinet as well as an impromptu speech by Chief Buthelezi, which appeared to be solely for the benefit of the New Zealander.

The comments and discussion around the lunch table gave us the distinct impression that the Inkatha Freedom Party was not going to be marginalised by the ANC, even if it involved bloodshed.

Chief Buthelezi's mini-speech made reflective references to the 'Zulu Empire' and there was a definite feeling of nationalism being stirred up in the room.

When Ray and our small group boarded the plane for our return flight to Johannesburg, we were in little doubt that Chief Buthelezi and his Inkatha Freedom Party were still a force to be reckoned with, but we were troubled by the degree of bitterness that seemed to have soaked into the ethos of those we had spoken to. This assessment was, sadly, not out of line, as Ray was to learn in the weeks and months that lay ahead when he became more intimately involved with the peace process.

The most positive news that Ray was able to bring back was the fact that the Rustenburg Committee, at this moment in time, looked a good bet for convening a second or follow-up peace conference to the Pretoria event, which was still to happen!

The feeling, among many, was that the Pretoria Peace Summit was now a nuisance, but in order to save face for the President it had to go ahead. And there was always the outside chance that something constructive might be achieved at the conference. But any hope of this being achieved was scuttled when the Government surprisingly announced that the Peace Summit would be open to the media and that they would be free to report on the events as they unfolded.

That was great news for the media, who felt that because of the obvious public concern on the issue of violence, which was touching all aspects of the nation, it should be freely reported. But it was a major blunder because most of the people and organisations who made public speeches played to the media, airing grievances and taking pot-shots at political opponents, and the main issues were sidelined.

However, it was a valuable lesson for those who would be responsible for getting the peace train back on track. In the meantime the Pretoria Summit had to run its fateful course.

The Summit was held on Friday and Saturday, May 24–25, 1991 at the CSIR convention centre in Johannesburg. Ray wanted me to accompany him, but I could not get an official invitation. However, I managed to bully my way in as a media representative.

When we arrived at the convention centre it was undoubtedly a Who's Who of moderates, with a few Right-Wingers to flavour the meeting. The absence of the Liberation movements, in particular the ANC, was so obvious that as the day proceeded it was apparent to all that very little would be achieved at this much-vaunted Peace Summit.

As Ray and I mingled in the vast foyer there was a flurry at the main entrance when the Inkatha Freedom Party delegation, led by Chief Buthelezi waving his traditional bead-embroidered baton, arrived. Besides their political delegation another entourage escorted the King of the Zulus, His Highness Goodwill Zwelethini.

Pushing through the babbling delegates Ray caught Chief Buthelezi's attention and exchanged a few words. Sadly, a lot of negativity still existed towards the Rustenburg Committee proposal, because of the connection with the South African Council of Churches.

Ray took his seat in the convention hall and I was banished to the media centre where I followed the proceedings on closed-circuit television, wondering whether it was worth our while to be there at all.

The conference then unfolded into a series of speeches and declarations by political leaders, academics and some business bosses and a few churchmen. Ray spoke once, commending the good offices of the Rustenburg Committee, a suggestion formally proposed later in the proceedings by Professor Heyns.

At a final general session, President de Klerk ventured to sum up and to give some direction to a group of leaders who seemed largely frustrated by the lack of concrete proposals to find solutions to the unrest in the country. All that had been achieved was to provide a platform for a variety of leaders, many from the minor league, to air their grievances with the hope that they would get some media coverage and gratify their constituents.

The best that President de Klerk could come up with was the obvious, and that was the possibility of a further conference which would embrace the ANC and others! For this purpose he called on Dr Louw Alberts to act as an emissary and to try and see how a future conference could be convened.

The Monday following the Summit saw Ray sacrificing his day off to rush off to Khotso House in Marshall Street Johannesburg, to a hastily convened meeting in Frank Chikane's office. Also at the meeting were Louw Alberts, Johan Heyns and myself. Dr Alberts, explaining his brief from President de Klerk, asked for 'quiet consultation and confidentiality' in whatever role the churchmen agreed to play.

Having experienced the frustrations of trying to rescue the previous peace meeting, Frank Chikane was forthright in his belief that the church could pull off a follow-up conference.

Always soft-spoken, Chikane noted that the 'world is waiting to hear . . .' And what was the world going to hear from the church? A rustle of bishops' skirts scurrying to prayer, or would they hear the tramping of boots as the army of Christ strode boldly onto the battlefield?

Ray was adamant that this was not only the church's great opportunity to take the lead in the nation, but that only the church could, in fact, make a peace conference work. The meeting, which lasted an hour, got straight to the bottom line, and it was decided in Khotso House on that autumn afternoon in May that the church would act as the catalyst; also that the ranks of a possible Facilitating Committee should be broadened to include other religious and business leaders.

The inclusion of business leaders was seen as important because the commercial and industrial sectors were fairly neutral and, of course, the economy was being adversely affected by the unrest and violence, making investments and future expansion extremely risky. It happened now that the Rustenburg Committee, which was mandated to meet as many political leaders as possible and formally listen to comment on the Rustenburg Declaration, was suddenly given an appointment with Chief Buthelezi.

The only difficulty was that the meeting had to be held at the Chief's offices in Ulundi, and as there is no regular commercial airline serving the area it meant chartering a plane. The coffers of the Rustenburg Committee were almost depleted and the cost of hiring a plane made it difficult. However, realising how important the appointment was in view of the need to seek for peace, Ray got the Rhema Church to sponsor the charter flight.

The plane trundled down the runway and clawed its way into the thin, high-veld atmosphere on Monday morning, June 3. The cabin was full with seven members of the Rustenburg Committee and I shared the cockpit with the pilot.

On arrival, we learnt to our disappointment that Chief Buthelezi was involved in presenting a bill in the legislative assembly and would not be meeting with us. However, we were to meet with other top-ranking officials. Past grievances were aired and it was again apparent that the Zulu officials chose to see the Rustenburg Committee simply as an extension of the South African Council of Churches and disregarded the Pentecostal, evangelical and Dutch Reformed Church representation.

Despite the differences, a spirit of tolerance did prevail and Chief Buthelezi joined the group for lunch. The meeting continued for some while after lunch, followed by a media conference.

When the Rustenburg party trooped across the runway apron to climb aboard the plane there was a certain weariness in their steps. It had been a tiresome day and was a clear warning sign that any future peace negotiations or constitutional talks were going to be arduous and exhausting. The quest for peace in South Africa looked almost impossible. In fact, without divine intervention it did not look worthwhile pursuing.

During the eighty-minute return flight the Rustenburg Committee got into huddle in the cramped confines of the cabin, and as the plane began its descent and the outline of Johannesburg etched the horizon against a fiery orange sunset, the churchmen vowed to stay in the peace process. They realised that they, as the Rustenburg Committee, could never pull it off, but Frank Chikane, Louw Alberts, Professor Heyns and Ray McCauley committed themselves to follow up practically on their earlier meeting in Khotso House and to form a broad-based church/business alliance to facilitate the peace process.

A meeting of the newly formed Facilitating Committee was set soon after at the head offices of the major industrial company Barlow Rand, in Sandton. The office complex, set in lush garden surrounds called Barlow Park, would for the next fourteen weeks become so familiar that the Facilitating Committee could not have been blamed for thinking it was also their place of work.

June 22 was fixed for the next peace conference which would be a one-day event and held at the Barlow Park conference centre. Unlike the Government-convened Peace Summit in Pretoria, the Facilitating Committee decided to keep the media out of the meeting and to keep the delegations as small as possible. It was also agreed that the June 22 meeting would not attempt to bring together the major political leaders like President de Klerk, Nelson Mandela or Chief Buthelezi. Instead high-ranking deputies were to be invited. The plan was to use the meeting as a think tank, getting wide participation from delegates and then sifting through the ideas and suggestions and build on that for a possible third conference.

The exclusion of the media would ensure that delegates came to the conference with positive ideas and left behind their fault-finding speeches and hackneyed political slogans.

Another feature, developed by the Facilitating Committee, was the concept of joint chairmen, one Black and one White, one businessman and one churchman.

The Facilitating Committee were all smiles when it was confirmed that the three major parties, the Government, the ANC and the Inkatha Freedom Party, would attend. Various other smaller parties from the Liberation wing as well as from the status quo accepted invitations. But there was a negative response from the Right-Wing political groups. Although disappointed at failing at this hurdle the Facilitating Committee went confidently into the Barlow Park conference.

Ray and I arrived, wondering just how successful the exercise would be, and earnestly prayed that it would not be as depressing as the recent Pretoria Summit.

Although the media were excluded from the conference it had been agreed to allow TV cameramen and photographers a pre-meeting photo-session and some brief interviews with some of the participants. The Facilitating Committee and other delegates were besieged by reporters and camera people, with the international media very prominent. It was evident that the conference was going to get high-profile treatment.

Ray found himself moving in a new environment and something of a stranger among the political, trade union and business personalities of the land. True, he had met casually with some of the prominent leaders, but mostly within the confines of official occasions. Because of frequent media coverage, both in print and television, Ray's face was reasonably familiar to many of the delegates, but I could sense a curiosity factor from many who wondered what a Bible-thumping preacher was doing at such an occasion.

They soon found out. Ray had been selected to open the meeting in prayer, and I had carefully briefed him so that he would not lapse into a Rhema pulpit prayer, but rather a prayer that would be sensitive to the needs of the conference. He carried it off with flying colours. He made some short, pertinent opening remarks, prayed a brief but touching prayer, and retired to his chair next to the other members of the Facilitating Committee, which were facing the nearly 120 delegates.

Although the spiritual input seemed so small and insignificant, specially for those of the strong evangelical/Pentecostal ilk, it was, as we were to find out over the next weeks, remarkable just how it did influence and touch the hearts of many people.

At the close of the Barlow Park conference, a prominent South African industrialist strode across to me and remarked: 'Your man Ray surprised me with his prayer this afternoon. I've really seen him in a new light. I might even come to your church.' That comment underscored again just how misinformed people do become and how they are influenced by casual media reports and, sadly, wild gossip.

The conference, brilliantly chaired by Bishop Tutu when he got his opportunity to conduct the proceedings, went on to produce in a few hours what the Pretoria Summit failed to do in two days. Delegates stood up in rapid-fire succession and nailed the main issues and gave possible ways of finding solutions. The giant trade union group 'Cosatu' (Congress of South African Trade

Ray with Bishop Desmond Tutu

Unions) listed proposals that afternoon which eventually became key components of the Peace Accord.

A common thought from delegates was the urgent need for everyone to make a solemn commitment to peace, but also to set up codes of conduct for police and political parties and for the establishment of a 'peace secretariat' and other mechanisms which would practically monitor the unrest at grassroots level.

By the time the tea-break arrived there was consensus on what needed to be done. Now came the decision of how it was to be implemented—and, of course, by whom?

Although the meeting struggled for some while and looked like hitting a brickwall when the Pan African Congress (PAC) made it clear it would not join any committee which included the Government, Mr Zach de Beer, leader of the Democratic Party in the South African parliament, then made an inspiring and decisive contribution when he said that his party would stand down and would not seek to be included in any future committee charged with following through the Barlow Park proposals.

The logjam was suddenly broken, because other lesser political groups began to drop their ideas of being in on the action and within a short while the 'Preparatory Peace Committee', as it was to become, took shape.

There was also a strong plea by Mr Zach de Beer for the present Facilitating Committee to continue, and he made special reference to the church, saying that they needed to be involved. And so a new committee, consisting of the existing Facilitating Committee, the Government and the National Party, the Inkatha Freedom Party and an ANC alliance, was formed.

Following on the magnanimous offer of the DP to withdraw, the ANC grouping agreed to a compromise which brought about the ANC alliance, which meant one ANC member, one South African Communist Party member, and one trade union member from Cosatu.

The charge of the new committee was plain and concise. They were to continue the peace process, plan a future peace summit and establish working groups to address specific issues highlighted during the afternoon, including items earmarked at the Pretoria Summit.

I drove Ray home that evening and he was confident that something positive had been accomplished and that it was now up to the politicians and their aides to get the job done.

13

Stop the Violence

The Barlow Park conference certainly put out some hopeful signals to the country, and there was every reason to be confident because the intensity and ugliness of the violence made any small forward step seem like a giant leap.

The newly formed Preparatory Committee did not waste any time in calling their first meeting. It was held the following Monday evening, again at Barlow Park. Ray was unable to attend because of church matters and so I deputised for him.

As we took our seats there was a freshness in the air and a willingness to get to grips with the issue of violence and the meeting forged ahead with its agenda. We agreed that too much hot air had already been expended and that more action and fewer words were needed, especially for the large numbers of deaths and resulting hurt caused to widows and orphans and families.

Five Task Groups were appointed and it was agreed

that the business/churchman formula would continue, with this duo being the convenors of each Task Group.

It so happened that, in Ray's absence, I was paired with Bobby Godsell of Anglo-American and assigned to Task Group Four, which, as I was to learn shortly, had a mammoth commission placed on its shoulders. The next day when I gave Ray a report-back on the evening's meeting he didn't respond too happily about being a convenor of a highly technical Task Group.

Ray's whole style of leadership is based on the very practical premise of 'what's the bottom line?'. In the confines of church leadership that tends to work reasonably well but, as Ray was learning, 'bottom lines' seldom materialised when politicians were involved in debates. Every word, every gesture, every compromise was a cover-up for another devious ploy, which is the armour of any self-respecting politician.

In the church arena and especially on his own turf, it is relatively easy for Ray to cut to the bone. He hears what he needs to hear and then makes his decision. Now, in the peace process, he found himself eclipsed by people who were masters of political debate. Not that he could not grasp the manipulative undertones going on, but he found himself frustrated because he realised that in this league he could not have the final say.

So I realised that I would have to endure the arduous hours of political in-fighting and negotiating which would emanate from the Task Group. There was no way that Ray would sit calmly through all the complex debate of Standing Commissions on Law and Order, the drafting of documents for the establishment of peace secretariats, regional committees and regional criminal courts, which were some of the subjects assigned to Task Group Four!

I went back to my office and took a deep breath. I

was now solemnly deputised to represent Ray on the Task Group. Not only would I have to survive the onerous meetings that lay ahead, but I would have to attempt to digest them into 'bottom-line' reports of less than a page so as to keep Ray up to date on the peace process!

It was laborious work being on that Task Group, but I gained great admiration for Bobby Godsell and his incisive way of assisting the political players. I hope that Ray's and my prayers had something to do with it!

At the first session of Task Group Four, the Government representatives introduced a document proposing ways and means of monitoring the violence, and practical suggestions to establish controls and mechanism right down to the grassroots level.

The various Task Groups were now feverishly at work with sporadic meetings of the Preparatory Committee being held to gauge the speed with which the process was going forward. Unfortunately Ray had to miss a few meetings because of two ministry trips overseas, one to America in July, and the other to Czechoslovakia in August.

Most heartening to see was the determination of the three political parties to work something out. As the process began to evolve it became plain that we were heading towards a climactic event, and it was for the Preparatory Committee to decide what this event would be.

The media were by now fascinated with the operation and an atmosphere was being created for the public to expect something pivotal from the peace process.

The thought of a third conference was quickly discarded and the concept of a symbolic event emerged. It became obvious from the work being done by the Task Groups that a document of serious content was in the making. Thus the Peace Accord was born.

In rough detail the committee agreed to the idea of the leaders of the three major parties signing the Peace Accord, and as many other political, trade union, business and church leaders as possible would be encouraged to lend their signature to the Accord.

Meanwhile the reality was that the killing continued, with violent outbursts in Natal and on the Witwatersrand. But the focus on the peace process became even sharper. The ANC began to press for a signing of the Peace Accord as soon as possible, suggesting dates in August. However, September 14 was agreed upon. It would be called a Peace Convention and would include the signing of the Peace Accord.

It was planned to make it a massive public event, with the media encouraged to give it live coverage. It was to be seen as an historic milestone in the life of the nation. Despite the apparent ease with which the process was rolling along, there were some nasty bumps and hurdles to overcome before September 14.

On August 14 the original Facilitating Committee was summoned to an emergency meeting at Mr John Hall's office at Barlow Park. Ray was able to attend and when we walked into the room it was clear, from the anxious faces and chatter, that something serious had happened. Brief report-backs indicated that the parties were becoming deadlocked on certain issues.

The Government group wanted certain matters resolved with the ANC, and was trying to set conditions, which were being linked to previous talks the two parties had held on constitutional affairs. The Inkatha Freedom Party was differing seriously on interpretations of clauses and one in particular, on 'dangerous weapons', was becoming an aggravating thorn in everyone's side.

The Facilitating Committee bandied around some

thoughts and one solution was to form a sub-committee to investigate the matter further.

Ray sat on a leather couch, listening and interjecting occasionally, and then fell silent as he let the rest of the committee members argue the pros and cons. Then he leaned forward on his seat and, waving his arm, got the opportunity to speak. His outburst—that is the only way to describe it—chided the committee members for taking such a negative attitude.

He spelt out in very plain terms that if the peace process failed at this point then 'we have failed totally'. 'Don't think we've done anything great here, because we haven't. And if we don't keep this thing going, then we've missed it totally. We've got to make it work and we've got to make the parties see that.'

Spoken with all his evangelistic fervour, this jolted the committee members into momentary silence. Then one member, his ego shaken, retorted that he didn't think the committee had done such a bad job—after all it had got to this point.

However, Ray's boldness and typical gutline emphasis registered with the majority of the committee, who mentally regrouped. I was amazed how the atmosphere of the room was transformed. The despondency lifted and the hazy thinking was blown away with a determined mood to keep the peace train on the tracks.

Separate consultation with the parties, amazingly, resolved the issues. It was decided that the niggling matters between ANC and Government, which arose out of bilateral talks, should not be introduced into the peace process.

The issue of 'cultural or dangerous weapons' was, of course, very much part of the peace initiative and a highly volatile subject. The parties were persuaded not to get bogged down on this one issue, but to press forward on matters that could be agreed upon and to continue debating the weapons question.

And so the peace initiative momentum was maintained, although there were by now continual verbal skirmishes occurring between the ANC and Buthelezi's Inkatha Freedom Party.

Right at the start of the peace initiative the Inkatha Freedom Party had requested the need for simultaneous bilateral talks in order to tidy up outstanding business between the two parties. As the weeks rushed by, these talks failed to materialise and often became a matter of contention during the peace process. The friction between the ANC and Inkatha was always apparent, and unknown to the media at the time the peace process came close to being derailed on several occasions.

Ray was repeatedly telephoned from Richards Bay, in Natal, by Mr Walter Fellgate, senior member of the Inkatha Freedom Party negotiating team. Fellgate, short in stature and pugnacious and bustling in character, constantly harped on about what he perceived was shoddy treatment of his party.

There was an obvious mistrust, not only of the ANC, but also of the church, especially of the involvement of Bishop Tutu and Frank Chikane. The impression was sometimes given that the Inkatha officials were being paralysed by past anger and mistreatment, which stopped them grasping the opportunities of the present and the future.

Ray would often come through to my office after one of the many phone calls from Fellgate, wringing his hands and wondering whether his assurances that the Inkatha Freedom Party would get a fair deal would satisfy the rulers in Ulundi.

Despite these vexing challenges Ray was able to cool the temperature and it was gratifying to see the Inkatha

Freedom Party delegates continue doggedly in the process.

The whole peace process got a severe jolt when a newspaper revealed that the Government had secretly funded the Inkatha Freedom Party for the staging of certain political rallies. What aggravated the covert operation was the fact that the funds had been channelled to Inkatha via the South African Police.

Ray was in Oslo at the time of what became billed as 'Inkathagate', and had an hour-long interview with Mr Jan Egeland, first secretary to the Norwegian Minister of Foreign Affairs. The Norwegian Government, like most other Western countries, were watching closely the efforts of the peace initiative, because they saw it as part of the process towards true political freedom for Black people.

Ray was told that the Norwegian government was keen to drop sanctions against South Africa and was preparing to open a full embassy in Pretoria, but viewed the Inkathagate scandal in a serious light. Because he was involved intimately with the peace initiative, Ray was able to assure the Foreign Affairs official that, despite the seriousness of the situation, he was sure that President de Klerk and Chief Buthelezi would deal decisively with the matter.

Chief Buthelezi, critically embarrassed by the covert funding, ensured that action was taken and some heads rolled. President de Klerk, also besmirched, especially in the light of an earlier pronouncement that all secret funding by Government departments had been terminated, read the riot act to his lieutenants.

In an attempt to bury the issue Chief Buthelezi ordered that the money, R250,000 (£50,000), be repaid to the South African Government.

Although there was a considerable public debate about

the secret funding it did not affect the peace process. In fact, on the day that the Inkatha chairman Dr Frank Mdlalose handed over the cheque there was a meeting of the Peace Committee at Barlow Park and Communist Party representative Mr Aziz Pahad could not help remarking towards the end of the evening how amazing it was that the funding scandal had in no way impinged on the business of the Peace Committee.

But, as the September 14 Peace Accord day loomed closer, the frustrations of the arduous and difficult negotiations began to take their toll on all those involved with the Peace Accord. On Wednesday, September 11, three days before the historic Peace Accord was to be signed, a major hitch arose. Ironically, it was sparked off by the original Facilitating Committee.

The final touches to the document were being debated while a special media committee was polishing up the final arrangements for the big day, which was planned as a media spectacular with as many press present as Peace delegates.

One of the issues under discussion was the choice of chairmanship for the historic day. Various formulas were proposed, including the idea of alternating joint chairmen. There had been discussion among the churchmen on the committee, and during the day Ray had been phoned and asked what he thought about the idea of having Bishop Tutu as the chairman for the day.

In view of the fact that the day was to be extremely symbolic, with the three major political leaders signing the Peace Accord, it seemed only natural that a former Nobel Peace prize winner would add to the symbolic dressing of the event.

Ray, who was conducting a four-day seminar on the gifts of the Holy Spirit, could not attend, so I was briefed to support the nomination of Bishop Tutu. The evening meeting was rattling along with only a few minor rumbles ... and then the matter of the chairmanship came up.

The Inkatha Freedom Party threw a wildcard on the table when they proposed Bishop Stanley Mgoba, the presiding head of the Methodist Church. I was quickly out of the starting blocks and ended up being the person who nominated Bishop Tutu. There was great irony in this because of the past misunderstandings and strange perceptions that so many charismatics and Pentecostals held about the Bishop, and he of us.

Sensing that the debate could get ugly, Bishop Tutu excused himself from the room and then the debate began. The ANC and the Government delegates took a backseat during most of the discussion, and it was left to the Inkatha Freedom Party and the Facilitating Committee to argue the issue out.

In frustration it was agreed to call off the debate and the Facilitating Committee was asked to meet separately to see how the matter could be resolved.

We withdrew to John Hall's office and glumly took stock of what had happened. There was an air of despair among the committee who had amazingly brought together the parties and now appeared to have wrecked its own good work.

Frank Chikane, who had been sorely slighted on several occasions that evening and at previous meetings by the Inkatha Freedom Party delegation, opened up his heart. Usually so certain of himself and always composed, even when under verbal attack, Frank poured out the frustrations that were tearing at him. He was an exhausted man, having worked tirelessly for the past five months on trying to end the violence. He'd personally seen much of the carnage and in one frightening incident had nearly become a victim himself when surrounded by a bloodthirsty mob of squatters in Soweto.

Chikane candidly told his colleagues he could no longer tolerate the insults and lack of appreciation. Professor Heyns offered words of solace and comfort to Frank, endeavouring to encourage him.

Bishop Mgojo spoke about the hurt caused to Bishop Tutu and then the committee slowly came around to trying to find a solution. They didn't find one that evening and when we left, well after midnight, the only escape hatch left was the possibility of a dash to Ulundi to speak to Chief Buthelezi.

I telephoned Ray early on Thursday morning to brief him on the situation and to alert him to be ready to fly to Natal for a meeting with Chief Buthelezi.

Just before 10 o'clock I received a call at my office from Sean Cleary who was speeding along in his car to the Lanseria airport. Contact had been made with Chief Buthelezi and he was prepared to meet with a delegation, if they could come to the small town of Mandini where he was speaking at a function.

Facilitating Committee chairman John Hall arranged for a Barlow Rand company jet to be made available, and he and Cleary were now driving to the airport.

I had strongly argued for Ray to be included in any last-minute delegation to see Chief Buthelezi, and Cleary had promised to call me if it was arranged. So I immediately phoned Ray who was sitting in his family room, dressed in a suit and ready to go. He rushed out by car to catch the flight.

In the meantime I had lost contact with Cleary's carphone and wasn't sure he had got my final confirmation that Ray was on his way to the airport. I had a disquieting vision of Ray panting down the runway and the jet hurtling off into space, and knowing his temperament I would have to take the first flight to China!

So I got my secretary, Maureen, to contact the Airport Control Tower and inform them that a Reverend Ray McCauley would be a passenger on the flight which was warming up to take off for Zululand and that it must not leave without him. An hour passed by and only then did I breathe easier, knowing that Ray was definitely on his way to see Buthelezi.

When the trio—Hall, Cleary and Ray—landed they were taken to a warehouse where Chief Buthelezi left the meeting he was involved in to meet privately with the peace envoys.

It was a warm, sultry day, but the mood in the room was definitely a bit frosty. It was plain to the three that there was no way Chief Buthelezi would attend the Peace Accord, which was two days away, if Bishop Tutu was chairman. It was non-negotiable. Only the previous evening he had given an interview to a BBC correspondent in which he indicated serious doubts about the validity of the Peace Accord.

Although the meeting was always cordial, it was plain that Chief Buthelezi's difficulty was not only the Tutu issue, but the Peace Accord concept itself. He seemed to doubt whether it could be properly implemented. Citing previous accords which had been drawn up between Inkatha and the ANC in Natal, he complained bitterly that nothing had changed. The killing and destruction continued.

Ray was asked to pray. Although usually brief he decided that it was going to be a bit longer than usual. Besides the prayer Ray also made a plea from his own heart for the Chief to give the Peace Accord a chance.

After an anxious hour of talks and prayer Chief Buthelezi gave the trio his assurance that he would attend the Peace Accord so long as Bishop Tutu was not the chairman. He did concede that the Bishop could close the meeting in prayer.

The Chief's given reason for his opposition to Tutu was that churchmen should keep within their boundaries and not cross over into the political domain, but it was all right for a businessman to chair the Saturday meeting.

Immensely relieved, the trio flew back, hoping that Bishop Tutu would not be too greatly offended and would be willing to do the closing prayer at the Peace Accord. When contacted, the Bishop—well aware of how sensitive the situation was becoming and not wanting to be a stumbling block—gracefully stepped down.

The stage was now set.

14

History Is Made

That same Thursday evening I again deputised for Ray as he continued conducting a highly successful and well-attended seminar on the Holy Spirit. While 2,000 of the Rhema congregation hungrily fed on the word of God, I found myself munching sausage rolls and involved in the final desperate hours to get the Peace Accord finalised.

The 'cultural weapons' issue was prominently back in focus with the ANC and Inkatha deadlocked. The Government and the ANC were nitpicking at words in another document, and the night wore on and on.

I got thrust onto a special media committee which was to assist with the organising of the press for the big day. It was well after midnight when I wearily drove home, but back at Barlow Park the parties were playing a waiting game with each other to see who could stay awake and alert the longest and not blunder into a concession which would give the other the upper hand.

On the next day, Friday, I went to the five-star Carlton Hotel in the centre of Johannesburg for a media briefing session, and learnt that the 'cultural weapons' clause in the Peace Accord had only been resolved just after noon. The rush was now on to get the actual Peace Accord document typed up and printed in time for the following morning.

Saturday morning, September 14. I arrived at the Carlton Hotel just after 6.00 am because I was to help with the registration of the media and also make sure that the seating arrangements for the Facilitating Committee, the churchmen in particular, were right. I was amazed when I got to the hotel and made my way from the basement to the main convention hall without once going through a security check. I was not wearing an identity badge and walked into the empty hall which was laid out and ready for the event, scheduled to begin at 8.00 am. I juggled a couple of place names around so that Ray was not isolated from Chikane and Tutu, whom he had become to appreciate and to enjoy.

The media, local and international, saturated the convention centre. The South African Broadcasting Corporation provided non-stop, live coverage on one of their spare transmitters. All of the overseas TV crews were in attendance and on their arrival, delegates were besieged by popping flashlights and jostling cameramen. The centre had a gala atmosphere.

It was easy to tell when Nelson Mandela arrived. The media centre emptied as though a giant vacuum had sucked them out of the area and deposited them in a jumbled heap at the head of the narrow escalator which transported Mr Mandela upwards.

Then President de Klerk and other leading figures streamed in, but no Chief Buthelezi. Rumours flitted around that he wasn't coming. The situation was further aggravated by the arrival of a large contingent of Zulus who had flooded the street in front of the hotel, heightening the tension by their blatant display of sticks, spears and other sharpened instruments.

Further rumours appeared that there was an ANC support group marching towards the hotel, which was now tightly ringed by police vehicles and heavily armed security forces.

The Peace Accord Day looked like deteriorating into a battle.

The King of the Zulus arrived with his entourage. This had been the centre of an argument during the build-up to the day, but had been resolved by an ANC compromise.

Then Chief Buthelezi arrived. He had broken his reading glasses the previous evening and there had been a frenzied dash in the morning to get them fixed, as he could not go to the Peace Accord without them! So the convention hall settled down with the three major political players together in the room.

Despite its patchy last two weeks, the Facilitating Committee could take some pleasure in their achievement, and Ray felt a definite sense of divine fulfilment, since responding to the still quiet voice in his car nearly four months earlier, which had catapulted him firmly onto the national platform as a church leader with something relevant to contribute to the New South Africa.

The meeting, chaired by John Hall, ran its course, with members of the Facilitating Committee giving short report and summaries of the documents.

Meanwhile, the Zulu impi outside the hotel had swollen in numbers, and I could see some of the mob swigging bottles of alcohol. This demonstration was, of course, getting brilliant TV coverage from the multitude of cameramen, who were all alert to the possibility of violence breaking out and of getting their pictures flashed across the TV screens of the world.

The official IFP delegation to the Peace Accord denied knowledge of any planned demonstration and seemingly did not see it as a threat to the convention.

Ray and some of the church leaders considered challenging Chief Buthelezi to go out and dismiss the mob, but it was President de Klerk who went across to the Chief and personally asked him to intervene and send the demonstrators home. This was done during the lunch break and the crowd, happy to have been addressed briefly by Chief Buthelezi, dispersed peacefully.

When the delegates returned from lunch the convention hall had been enlarged by removing the massive partitioning wall which separated the media centre from the delegates' venue. Now it was one huge hall with chairs laid out on the raised stage and a podium in place on which the three leaders would sign, and then other political groups and organisations would follow suit.

There was a forest of TV cameras facing the platform, with the delegates seated at the back of the media teams. For this occasion the media had a grandstand view of the historic event that was about to happen.

The three leaders sat next to each other on the front of the stage. Mr Mandela sat in the middle with President de Klerk on his right and Chief Buthelezi on his left. All three wore dark suits, although Mr Mandela, with a blue tie and blue-and-white striped shirt, took the honours for sartorial elegance, marred maybe because he insisted on wearing his name tag badge, unlike the other two leaders.

First up to sign the Peace Accord was Chief Buthelezi, and as the TV lights flared brightly and the cameras focused he began by first reading the account of the creation from the opening chapter of Genesis.

The Chief's speech carried heavy religious tones, with reference to the Lord Jesus Christ and a firm commitment of himself and his party to uphold the Peace Accord. He ended off his speech by adding that he was stretching out his hand to the ANC, and looked forward to the time when relationships with the ANC would be normalised. As he signed and came back to his seat, Mr Mandela nodded his head and acknowledged Chief Buthelezi.

Under the eye of the international media, every gesture, every movement of head or glint in the eye was being captured by the TV cameras.

When his turn came, Mr Mandela, stately and dignified, remarked that 'signatures alone cannot light the path of peace', and he pleaded for the 'warmongers' to be exposed. Then it was President de Klerk's turn to sign. Then he remarked in his speech that the Peace Accord was a 'living document'.

Ray and his colleagues on the Facilitating Committee sighed with relief as the three signatures were sealed on the Peace Accord, with very few of the delegates realising just how remarkable the achievement had been.

Mr Sam Motsuenyane, a business leader and a member of the Facilitating Committee who was the chairman for the afternoon, commented as he introduced Bishop Tutu to close the meeting that the peace initiative 'started with God, and God has done wonders . . .'.

Indeed the process, bumpy and rough as it may have been, was exceptional in its warmth of feeling and understanding. Yes, there had been problems, but they had been overcome by a common desire to do something positive about the violence.

The odd mixture of business and church leaders

interacting with politicians, whose economic and spiritual beliefs varied from capitalism to socialism and from Calvinism to Pentecostalism to atheism, was a remarkable feat.

Bobby Godsell, from Anglo-American, couldn't help remarking to me as we sat watching the signing what an amazing 'spiritual experience' the whole process had been to him.

Those were heartening words for Ray and his colleagues who had put in many hours and prayed many prayers for the success of the exercise. In fact thousands of Christians had been alerted across the country to pray and intercede for the peace talks, especially when it looked like disappearing into the quicksand of political expediency.

As Ray left the Carlton Hotel he wondered where the Lord would lead him next. He felt that his involvement had been divinely orchestrated. Whether he would be involved any further with the peace process, which would now flow out of the Peace Accord, was a matter for speculation.

He looked back on four hectic months during which he had spoken at major conventions and gospel crusades in America, Britain and Czechoslovakia. He was now preparing for a two-week speaking tour of America.

Besides the intense peculiarities of the peace initiative, there had also been the daily hurly-burly of running the church and the launching of a Christian Television Channel, known as CTV, which is dealt with in the next chapter. But it had been the peace initiative which held the high ground during those four months, and his involvement brought different reactions from several quarters.

From the more conservative-thinking Pentecostals, and even from within the congregation, came an anxiety

that Ray was being sucked into the vortex of politics—
a reaction he had experienced in 1990 when he was first
elected to the Rustenburg Committee. There were even
faint whispers within the staff that Ray should be
cautious about getting deeply involved with politicans.

Ray tries to be tolerant in his reaction to such
comments, which are sometimes expressed out of naïvety
and a lack of knowledge. To such he gives the simple
reply that Christians need to be light and salt in every
situation. Nor is he compromising his biblical beliefs: it
was the Lord Jesus himself who said, 'Blessed are
the peacemakers, for they shall be called the sons of
God.'

Some of the criticism was not the result of simple
ignorance, however, but from a sinister bias that is the
curse of South Africa. These are the racist bigots who
resent and despise Whites who are seen to be talking
with the 'enemy' which is perceived as being Mr Mandela
and the ANC.

Occasional, sniping criticism also comes from a
conservative band of Christians who feel that Ray should
take advantage of his favour with the political groups
to attack the moral decay in the nation.

These criticisms tend to irritate because Ray believes
he is not changing his very strong and fundamental
biblical beliefs. He is the first to acknowledge that there
is too much nudity being allowed on the TV screens and
in movie houses, and that divorce and drug addiction are
serious matters which need to be tackled. However, his
firm belief is that unless the violence is quenched,
allowing for a peaceful transition to some form of
majority rule, then all the moral concerns are side-issues.
His concern is that unless the church, and its leaders
in particular, don't roll up their sleeves and try to
bring about peace and reconciliation, then hatred and

bloodshed will be the order of the day for South Africa and the nation could become another Lebanon.

But besides the critics there were the sceptics among the general public and also among the clergy who could not conceive of Ray having a practical, down-to-earth social conscience!

There was another group—the curious, and among them were the media. The transformation of Ray from the locker room to the church pulpit was open for all to see and observe. The sharp, sceptical critics mellowed over the years as they saw Ray moving towards a genuine and meaningful role in the wider affairs of the country. Ray's involvement in the Rustenburg church conference dramatically altered the perception of many news people, and his involvement in the peace process further enhanced his public image.

Local and international newspapers and magazines wanted interviews, and their motivation was no longer to sensationalise doctrinal or money issues, but to question Ray on his views on the changing socio-political scene in South Africa.

It was, though, not only Ray's involvement in national issues which had boosted his national standing. There was his position as a leader of the IFCC and later on as president of the Pentecostal charismatic Fellowship of Southern Africa, which increased his credibility as a spokesman for a large group of Christians.

One additional factor in enlarging Ray's popularity has been television, and it was the inception of a Christian TV channel in South Africa that gained him wide exposure throughout the country.

15

Camera—Lights—Action!

South Africa is a country of many paradoxes. While the Government debased the human dignity of millions of people through apartheid, it still had some moral conscience when it came to the propagating of God's word.

The South African Broadcasting Corporation (SABC), a quasi-government organisation which controlled both radio and television in the country, has methodically produced religious programmes for all race groups and in a variety of languages, although there was a heavy bias towards the Dutch Reformed Church, and the ideological thread of racial segregation was promoted by only showing all-White or all-Black congregations when church services were first televised.

For years only 'tame' ministers were allowed on the airwaves and on TV programmes. Ministers who were thought to have a liberal, political inclination or were branded as promoters of a social gospel were kept off the SABC. The rules for any ministers invited by the SABC to preach on any radio or television programme were strict—no politics, no criticism of the Government, no criticism of other churches. The last mentioned is laughable because the Government used the SABC for decades to lambast churches and church leaders who opposed apartheid.

For years, too, there was a prohibition on Pentecostal churchmen. The highly influential Dutch Reformed Church had formally declared many years previously the Apostolic Faith Mission, the largest Pentecostal denomination, a cult. In fact, it was only in 1990 that a national synod assembly of the Dutch Reformed Church changed this decision and officially recognised the Apostolics as a bona fide Christian church!

So, although the word of God was propagated, and one has to be thankful for that mercy, it was in fact tightly controlled with the SABC setting itself up as the religious watchdog of the nation.

However, evangelicals and some Pentecostals like the Apostolic Faith Mission, kept lobbying and chipping away at the granite colossus of State-controlled religious broadcasts.

Slowly the barriers began to fall, especially on the Black programmes where more leeway was given, and although the occasional Pentecostal began to appear there were still severe restrictions. There was to be no mention of baptism in water by total immersion, and certainly no mention of speaking in tongues, the supernatural phenomenon which characterises the Pentecostal churches. The mention of healing and miracles was also frowned upon.

When television services from Pentecostal churches were first permitted a feeble attempt was made to try and avoid showing the congregation clapping and raising their hands in praise and adoration of the Lord.

Slowly the barriers began to crumble and Pentecostal churches and their pastors began to get a reasonable, if not equal opportunity to share the airwaves.

Then the 'Faith Movement' hit South Africa in 1978–79, and hundreds of independent churches, outside of any denominational control, began to mushroom across the country. Rhema, of course, was one of these new churches—and the largest and fastest-growing in the country. It was impossible to ignore Ray, and the pressure began to build up on the SABC to allow him onto their religious programmes. The pressure was boosted by the fact that a couple of producers in the SABC religious department were members at Rhema. They were longing to get an opportunity to show the South African public just what a Rhema church service looked and felt like.

Compared to traditional church services, especially those in the Dutch Reformed Church where the traditional singing of the Psalms is adhered to, a Rhema meeting with its big band and up tempo music would have looked like Pop Shop!

Not only was the traditional church service image threatened by Rhema, but Ray himself was regarded as too controversial. This stemmed mainly from a mis-understanding of the so-called prosperity doctrine. Although some individuals took the prosperity message out of context and began to use 'confession formulas', treating the word of God like a lucky packet, Ray had personally steered a middle road on this issue. Healing, in which Ray firmly believes, was another touchy subject with the SABC.

But the breaks eventually came Ray's way, beginning with an opportunity to do a couple of epilogues. There was a tangible nervousness on the part of the SABC religious bosses when Ray submitted his script for those early transmissions.

However, he played by the rules, avoiding any provocative statements and keeping safely to the Scriptures. The response from viewers was positive, the religious department chiefs sighed with relief and the first of several breakthroughs was made in the SABC.

Another milestone in the church's history came in 1989, when the SABC agreed to film a service from Rhema for Christmas Day. The filming was done in October and had to be held to a tight one-hour programme, Ray preaching a twenty-minute sermon.

The Rhema band excelled for the occasion, as did the special guest artists, and Ray preached a challenging message.

The service went out at noon on Christmas Day and must have startled some traditionalists with its up-tempo music and slick presentation. Many positive letters came in over the next couple of weeks.

Although Ray was not the darling of the SABC, or its religious department, they grudgingly admitted that he did have a substantial following and that the criticism from ultra-conservative religious quarters was outweighed by the good remarks received.

In the meanwhile, the beginnings of a development towards a separate Christian channel were being implemented.

Trinity Broadcasting Network, the largest gospel television organisation in the world, with low-powered transmitters in countries in every part of the earth, had established a small TV station in the Ciskei, one of the so-called 'homelands' established during the 'Grand Apartheid' era. Although the South African Government vigorously opposed any private radio or television stations within its own national borders, it did grant concessions in certain instances to broadcasters who were registered within 'Homelands'. And so Dr Paul Crouch had negotiated to establish a TBN station in the Ciskei, which served not only local inhabitants, but spilled over the borders to reach the South African port city of East London.

Dr Crouch, who has an unlimited vision for gospel television, began to make exploratory investigations into the possibility of getting a wider network which would one day serve the whole of South Africa. So began a long, drawn-out series of talks, meetings and negotiations, which fluctuated widely from extreme exhilaration to total doom.

A local business entrepreneur, Mr Walter Betschel, was appointed as the TBN representative and he began a succession of meetings with SABC officials, Government cabinet ministers and then with a Christian radio group called 'Radio Pulpit'. This group, which was supported and run by the Dutch Reformed Church, had established a Christian radio station some years before, and although initially limited in its transmission had made inroads and eventually secured the use of an FM channel.

When the rumour spread of a possible Christian TV channel Radio Pulpit became extremely interested and Ray, who is a personal friend of Dr Crouch, advised the TBN representative Walter Betschel to see what the possibilities were of TBN and Radio Pulpit joining forces to form the new Christian television channel.

Ray knew that the SABC and the Government would never agree to a wholly-owned American gospel station getting a licence for South Africa. However, if there was a joint venture with Radio Pulpit, whose strong Dutch Reformed Church influence would placate the Government, then there was a possibility of success.

The negotiations went round in circles. The Americans were prepared to finance the project and obviously wanted to maintain final control of the proposed new station. The Radio Pulpit negotiators insisted on a 51 per cent control, despite the fact that they were offering no money towards the project.

TBN magnanimously offered a 50–50 partnership, something which Dr Crouch has never done in any other country where he has negotiated similar gospel stations. Again the offer was rejected and the matter was stalemated.

Ray was in the background during most of these negotiations. He did not particularly want to get involved in the finer details of forming a TV channel. All he was interested in was getting time on the channel when it was formalised. Frankly, he was not concerned who ran the station.

With the TBN talks bogged down, the Radio Pulpit management took the initiative with a view to 'going it alone'. They held various meetings with churchmen, producers and technical people to test the possibilities. At the same time Walter Betschel of TBN, realising that Radio Pulpit would never become a minor partner with them, looked for a new South African ally. After talks with Ray and various other charismatic leaders a new company, called Christian Television (CTV), was formed. Ray was appointed to the CTV board.

Attempts were made by CTV to negotiate with the SABC, but there was dissatisfaction now when they and the Government realised that there were now two major players vying for a Christian channel—Radio Pulpit and the CTV-TBN alliance. Their response was to ask the two organisations to work together and then reapply for a licence.

Some efforts were made to reconcile the parties, but the Radio Pulpit hierarchy had become intransigent and, it seemed, obsessed with gaining total control of the airwaves.

The bottom line factor with Radio Pulpit (a common perception is that it emanated from the SABC and the Government) was the unthinkable thought of Pentecostal charismatics having free access to television and of tongue-talking preachers 'corrupting' the religious traditions of the Afrikaner people.

As the haggling went on, Ray began to despair of there ever being a Christian television channel, until he got a telephone call from Dr Willie van Rensburg, who was then Managing Director of Radio Pulpit. He invited Ray to come and meet him and have some discussion about Christian TV.

So Ray, myself and colleague Gordon Calmeyer travelled to the Pretoria headquarters for the meeting, which was cordial and friendly. Dr van Rensburg indicated that Radio Pulpit was very confident of getting a licence from the Government. This did not surprise us. What Radio Pulpit wanted to know from Ray was whether he would be interested in taking time on the channel if they secured the licence.

Although Ray was disappointed with the fact that a non-charismatic group would, it now seemed, have control, he maintained an open stance, saying that if time was available then Rhema would be interested.

We heard nothing more official from the Radio Pulpit management. Then Ray began to hear rumours that some of the congregation, who were involved in private television production houses, were being approached by Radio Pulpit, now using the name Good News TV.

It transpired that Good News TV (GNTV) had got a licence and been granted twenty-six hours of time on the SABC transmitters, and were now busy commissioning programmes.

Ray was flabbergasted. First, he knew nothing about the granting of the licence and neither had anyone from Radio Pulpit/Good News TV approached Rhema to supply any programme material. Yet they had blatantly approached presenters and producers in our congregation to make programmes.

When TBN's representative Walter Betschel heard about the granting of the licence, he too was upset. It was decided that the CTV board would seek an urgent meeting with the cabinet minister who was in charge of broadcasting.

This was arranged and CTV board members, Walter Betschel, Dr Izak Burger, moderator of the Apostolic Faith Mission, Pastor Ed Roebert, a co-leader of the IFCC with Ray, Pastor David Thebehali, an IFCC leader, Mr Martin Brink, an attorney, Ray and myself, trooped through the security checks at the government offices in Pretoria.

It was no meek and mild church delegation. As a group we were angry (we hoped it was holy anger!) at the perceived duplicity of the Government, the SABC and Radio Pulpit.

When Minister Mr Eugene Louw ushered us into a private boardroom the atmosphere in the room was as chilling as a morgue. A few pleasantries were muttered by each side and then Mr Betschel, as the group's main spokesman, got down to the heart of the matter, which was simply why had the Radio Pulpit people been favoured above CTV?

Minister Louw tried to throw a red herring into the discussion and mentioned an issue of litigation against

TBN in America, implying that this was a reasonable excuse for blocking CTV. It was explained that the alleged litigation was not criminal and was merely technical and, in fact, had been cleared up.

The conversation then focused on the pertinent issue of the granting of a licence to Radio Pulpit. Mr Louw said that he and the cabinet who had met to decide had been under the impression that all the parties, including the church groups on the CTV board, were committed to Radio Pulpit.

This disclosure amazed the CTV delegation, who quickly informed the minister of the true facts, that they had not been invited to participate, and that it was CTV's perception that the cabinet had not been apprised of all the facts when granting the licence.

Ray, infuriated by the disclosure, kept a tight control on himself as he explained how CTV had tried to unite with everyone, but that these efforts had been shunned. He then made a blunt attack on the Radio Pulpit philosophy, saying that the Dutch-Reformed-Church-orientated message would not find any credibility among the vast majority of Blacks. He was heartily endorsed in this sentiment by Dr Burger, who spoke in Afrikaans and clearly made the minister squirm at his frankness.

Ray cuttingly told the minister that he believed the Radio Pulpit attitude was the typical Dutch Reformed attitude of wanting to maintain a tight control on what went out on the airwaves. This was, in fact, a slap at the Government.

I was sitting next to Ray, astonished at how succinctly he was summing up the situation, but I got a bit concerned when he dropped a not too veiled threat to expose the duplicity of the Government, SABC and Radio Pulpit, to the newspapers.

Minister Eugene Louw gave every appearance of being

surprised by the revelations which our delegation imparted and, to his credit, gave a solemn assurance that he would take the matter to his cabinet colleagues at the soonest possible moment. After that he would call us to meet with him again.

As the CTV delegation walked out into the hot glare of a summery November afternoon, Ray was reasonably confident of a positive response from the Government.

Within weeks the CTV delegation was summoned to the minister's office. There was no hint of what decision we were going to hear. While the CTV delegation sat in a reception room, we speculated on what the minister's decision would be. Somehow, none of the members seemed over-optimistic, and by the time a secretary came to shuffle us through to the boardroom where we had met previously the CTV members had worked themselves into quite an aggressive mood. Any negative decision from the minister was going to be met with a stormy response.

Minister Louw settled himself at the head of the table, and as eight pairs of eyes glared towards him he calmly and softly told us that CTV had been granted permission to have an equal number of hours—twenty-six a month—as Good News Television.

The tension snapped, and there were smiles and grateful thanks exchanged and a silent prayer offered to the Lord who had indeed granted CTV favour in this situation.

There were, of course, restrictions. No criticism of other churches or debate on controversial matters of doctrine. No 'political' sermons and in fact, nothing that would rock the status quo of the SABC's Religious Department's code of conduct, which we already knew about.

Now the rush was on to get on the air. Ray, because

of the fluctuations of the situation, had wisely held back on investing in any major new equipment, making Rhema's video chief, Syd Huckfield, patch up the old cameras and make them work until there was some clarity on the Christian TV channel.

A target date was set for February 1991 to go on the air. It seemed a ridiculously short deadline to work to, but such was the enthusiasm that Rhema and the other CTV members blundered on. Delays in purchasing equipment and the preparation of programmes, however, soon brought everyone back to their senses, and a new launch date was set for Sunday, June 2.

From the beginning Ray wanted at least an hour a month, possibly more, and Rhema were allocated a programme every second week. The next decision for Ray was what time slot to aim at. The transmission times offered to CTV by the SABC were from 6.00 am until 10.00 am each Sunday morning.

When Ray attended a CTV Board meeting in the offices of Martin Brink, in Pretoria, when the allocation of time slots was to be decided, Ray surprised his colleagues by taking the early 7.00 am to 8.00 am time. His reasoning was simply that he did not want to clash with actual local church services. He was wary of creating an electronic church congregation, which might affect church attendance. During his frequent visits to America over the past ten years Ray has observed how Christian television has been abused by some people, and in many cases the authority and influence of the local church and the pastor have been undermined.

One recurring warning that came from the Government and the SABC when CTV got its licence was that there were to be no appeals for finance, an aspect of American Christian television which has been widely misused and exploited for selfish gain by some organisations. Ray and all the CTV members heartily agreed that begging for finances on TV was a definite 'no'.

However, although Ray was willing to comply with a ban on blatant soliciting of funds, he and CTV were unhappy about a restriction on advertising.

Initially the SABC shrewdly reserved the right to spot advertising for themselves. They were not only looking to make extra revenue out of the time they were selling to CTV, but were planning to wait and see what audience response would be like, and if it warranted it they were hoping to cash in on advertising for themselves.

This changed early in 1992 when the advertising embargo was lifted and CTV was permitted to canvass on the open market. But at first the financing of Christian television was entirely dependent upon churches raising their own funds, or finding sponsorship for their own programmes.

The canvassing of sponsors for specific programmes was a concession which the SABC had made to CTV. However, it did not open up the door to major advertisers, who were reluctant or shy to identify themselves too closely with a specific church. The later change in policy, however, may open better opportunities for CTV.

Ray initiated a meeting with local businessmen in the church and was able to get commitments of several thousand Rands, but nowhere near the figures which bigger, national companies pumped into secular TV programmes, and in particular to sports events.

The format of the Rhema programme was to be centred on the Sunday services, with Ray's sermon edited down to thirty minutes, a couple of music items and an actuality section which was developed by Ray's wife Lyndie, who adapted to the challenges of television with amazing swiftness.

The June 2 deadline came thundering along, with feverish efforts being made to put together a special programme for the launch day. There was a reshuffle in the administration of CTV, with Walter Betschel relinquishing his post as Acting General Manager. Louis Moller, who had been on the perimeter of earlier discussion about the possibilities of a Christian channel, was called in to fill the gap. Besides being an ordained Pentecostal minister, Moller was also a highly experienced executive TV producer and had been in partnership with the internationally known Bill Faure, who made the TV film epic *Shaka Zulu*.

Moller, now living and farming in the Mossel Bay area of the Eastern Cape, threw himself wholeheartedly into getting CTV on its feet. His grasp of the television industry was most welcome and together with his ex-business partner Bill Faure they put together an outstanding special for June 2.

It included interviews and good wishes for the new Christian channel from President de Klerk, various church leaders, businessmen, media and sports personalities and spliced in between were some prominent gospel musicians and singers, which gave the programme a slick, professional look. Charismatic Christian television had arrived, at last, in South Africa.

It was now over to the general public. The test of its acceptance or rejection was with the viewers.

An added bonus for CTV was the fact that it had beaten Good News TV and gone on air first. There was considerable irony in this fact, because although CTV was not consciously competing with Good News Television it had been expected that because of their long lead in getting the green light from the Government they would automatically beam their programmes first.

This was not to be, because they too had suffered

a minor management shake-up and only now were getting to grips with the costs involved in making TV programmes. Despite all their blustering and sometimes dubious tactics in securing Christian TV rights they had, in fact, exposed themselves as totally unprepared for Christian television. This strengthened the perception that their real motive was, in fact, to try and block the Pentecostal charismatic churches from gaining a foothold in national television.

When Good News TV eventually did come onto the air it was further embarrassed by being unable to take up all of its allocated time and having to purchase programmes from the Christian Broadcasting Network of America, whose founder Pat Robertson is a charismatic!

However, CTV and Good News TV, despite the grievances, maintained a cordial contact. But after only a couple of months Good News TV went off the air. The cost of programming had been too high for them to maintain.

They made a decision to leave TV to the CTV group and to concentrate on radio, through Radio Pulpit, with plans to expand that eventually to a twenty-four-hour service.

In the meanwhile CTV has established a niche, with a viewership of in excess of 200,000 each Sunday morning. Rhema's programme, despite its early time slot, has produced some outstanding results. On the first day over 100 telephone calls were received, with many first-time decisions made for the Lord. On one particular Sunday the local telephone exchange overloaded from a sudden deluge of phone calls at the conclusion of the Rhema programme. In an effort to avoid this sudden rush Rhema now scrolls a phone-in number at various times during the programme.

Voluntary phone counsellors fill every office in the Rhema Administration block on the Sundays when the church's programme is on TV. A network of counsellors has been organised through associate churches in most major cities across the country.

The response to Ray's programme has been outstanding and has given him another critical platform to speak out into the nation. Hundreds and possibly thousands of people, who would never come to the Rhema Church, have now been exposed to Ray's bold and pertinent preaching of the gospel.

Although no measurable growth in the local Rhema congregation can yet be attributed to television, there is little doubt that Ray is touching thousands of lives across the country.

Possibly just as important is the fact that many church leaders, Black and White, are listening to Ray's messages. This has been gauged by letters and comments Ray receives sometimes when visiting and speaking in other cities.

Although CTV has gained a strong and growing audience, its position in the future development of broadcasting seemed hazy as the political leaders began debating the future changes of the country.

One contentious area with the ANC and with all of the Liberation movements has been the State-control and influence over the national broadcaster. It is an issue which will be hotly debated by the political parties, and Christians are anxiously watching the outcome as to whether the CTV programmes will be threatened by the forthcoming shake-up of the national broadcaster. There is a solid lobby by some wanting to deregulate the airwaves, and the SABC has already taken positive steps towards privatising some of its channels.

There is also the reality that in the New South Africa

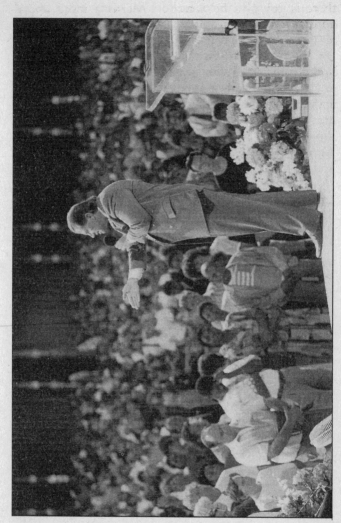

Rav's bold preaching (to Black and White) is now watched on TV as well

there is going to be a move towards a more liberal approach to religious affairs, meaning that other groups may challenge the church for air time.

CTV, though, is fast establishing itself as a Christian broadcaster, and with general acceptance of the programmes provided, it should be within their scope to maintain a vibrant gospel witness through television in the future.

16

Do You Support Reform?

As 1991 closed, Ray and Lyndie and eight-year-old son Joshua retreated to their holiday home on the Natal South Coast. It was a time to rest and gather strength for whatever the new year would bring. The previous two years had certainly been fast-paced for Ray and the church. But it was in keeping with the events that were taking place in the nation.

However, Ray's holiday was abruptly disturbed when he got news that an IFCC school in the small mining town of Klerksdorp had been bombed and badly damaged. Fortunately, the explosion happened in the early hours of the morning and no one was hurt.

It so happened that I too was on holiday on the South Coast, at a holiday resort nearby. I drove over to see Ray, knowing that he would want to issue a strong media statement.

With the help of some local people we found a word processor at the resort clubhouse and I pounded out a statement, while Ray, back at his holiday home, was unpacking a fax machine which he had brought with him—in case of emergencies.

Once we'd got the fax hooked up and Ray had approved the statement I faxed it to the various newspapers around the country. The bombing of the school made headline news in most national newspapers as well as featuring prominently on radio and television.

As the story unfolded a Right-Wing extremist group claimed responsibility for the bomb blast, which caused almost R1 million (£200,000) worth of damage. The reason for this savage act, which Ray described as 'cowardly', was because the school had a large number of Black pupils. Klerksdorp, with its dominant mining community and typical rural Afrikaans population, was strongly Right Wing.

The local town council was controlled by the Conservative Party, and since its establishment the multi-racial Christian school, called the Klerksdorp Christian Academy, had been a victim of harassment. The town council attempted to restrict the intake of pupils to Whites only and then, by manipulating municipal bylaws, tried to force the closure of the school.

All these efforts were met with staunch prayers and legal counter-attacks, until eventually an agreement was reached between the town council and the school management, which allowed the school to remain multi-racial, provided it did not contravene any basic municipal bylaws. It was seen as a victory for the concept of non-racist education, and also for the principle of sitting down peaceably and negotiating and understanding each party's point of view.

Sadly, there are elements in South African society which see little value in dialogue and negotiations around a table, and it was this extreme, militant group who bombed the school in mid-December 1991. During the month several other multi-racial education facilities were attacked and damaged by explosions.

Some of the perpetrators were caught by the police.

This incident, at the close of the year, was a hint of a growing militancy among Right Wingers against even charismatic Christian churches and their leaders.

During December another historic milestone was achieved with the formation of the Council for a Democratic South Africa, now known as Codesa.

Codesa was a natural follow-up to the National Peace Accord, only this body was charged with purely political matters, with the aim of charting the way forward to a new constitution and a new multi-racial government.

The participants were political organisations from the whole spectrum of the country, and included leaders from the so-called Homelands, or Bantustans, which had been part of the Grand Apartheid strategy of previous Nationalist Party Governments.

Unfortunately, none of the Right-Wing political parties, although invited, would join Codesa. They vehemently denounced President de Klerk for this role in forming Codesa and viewed it as a sellout of White South Africans.

The Conservative Party leader Dr Treurnicht and other Right-Wing leaders were disgusted by the fact that President de Klerk was now sitting down and negotiating the future of the country with what they still termed 'terrorists and atheists'. There were charges that the Afrikaners' culture was being betrayed, and their Christian heritage threatened.

This perception was enhanced when at the official opening ceremony of Codesa a Rabbi, a Muslim, a Hindu priest and a Christian opened the proceedings in prayer.

A similar thing had occurred at the signing of the Peace Accord, but did not draw much criticism.

However, the Codesa opening ceremony drew considerable hostility from the Right Wing and from fundamentalist Christians. It became one of several matters of contention during the blitzkrieg referendum campaign in March 1992. Many Christians felt it was a serious compromise to have people praying to false gods, especially on television in front of the whole nation.

As the first two months of 1992 galloped away, with Ray speaking at major conferences in Oslo and in Munich, and then returning for three stirring nights of gospel concerts with American singer Carman, the Black-on-Black violence continued.

On several occasions Ray bewailed the ineptness of the Peace Accord, as did other church and businessmen who had been a part of the peace initiative. However, the increase in violence could not be attributed solely to political motivations. Crime was soaring because of the millions of people who were out of work. There was also easy access to firearms, and it was said that an AK47 could be bought for as little as R500 (£100).

With Ray hoping to concentrate solely on the work of the ministry, and looking to make extensions to the building within the next eighteen months, it came as a surprise when he found himself pitched once again into a political whirlpool.

It came about when President de Klerk called for a referendum to be held on Tuesday, March 17. The referendum call caught most people by surprise, and many questioned the wisdom of the move.

The decision to call for a 'yes' or 'no' vote on reform came after a stunning defeat for de Klerk's National Party in the previously safe seat of Potchefstroom.

Although there had been predictions that Dr Treurnicht's Conservative Party might win the by-election by a narrow margin, no one expected them to win by such a large and convincing leeway. They turned a 2,000-odd vote defeat into a 2,500-vote victory.

President de Klerk and his National Party colleagues were clearly rattled and decided to call for the referendum in order to get a clear mandate from Whites to continue with the Codesa negotiations. The question they put to the nation was simply this: 'Do you support continuation of the reform process which the State President began on February 2 1990, and which is aimed at a new Constitution through negotiation?' Massive publicity campaigns were mounted and Mr de Klerk and Dr Treurnicht engaged in whirlwind, whistle-stop tours of towns and cities that smacked of American-style presidential elections.

Bitter words were exchanged during the public campaign, and the White population of South Africa had never been so divided in all its history. Unfortunately it rubbed off on the church.

Ray's involvement in the referendum started when wild allegations that the invisible marking of voters' hands (to guard against cheating) was in fact the 'Mark of the Beast'. Pentecostal fundamentalists, who seem to spend more time than most reading books on the 'end times', were adamant that this referendum marking was the beginning of the end as set out in the book of Revelation in the Bible.

The rumour was treated as a joke at first, but when Ray's secretary, Dyllis Rahme, began receiving calls and some reports appeared in newspapers it was felt that Ray should issue a public statement. Ray's statement, of course, refuted the notion of the 'Mark of the Beast' and urged all Christians to exercise their right to vote because there was a strong possibility that many Pentecostals would stay away from the ballot box.

Just as I was preparing to release Ray's press statement I received a telephone call from the cabinet minister, Mr Gene Louw, who said he was under the impression that Ray was urging Pentecostals not to vote! It seemed that someone was trying to sow discord. I read Ray's statement to the minister over the phone, and I could clearly hear his sigh of relief when he realised that Ray was calling on Christians to vote. Although the statement did not explicitly urge a 'yes' vote it was clearly biased towards it. The reason for hedging on the 'yes' vote was because of the negative feedback that we were hearing from Pentecostal Christians across the country. In addition several fundamentalist Christian newsletters were creating the strong impression that a 'yes' vote was tantamount to a vote for Marxism/Communism.

Rumours continued to reach our ears that Ray was not going to vote, and so he decided to come out publicly and declare that he was going to vote 'yes' and hoped that others would follow his lead.

As soon as the press release reached the newspapers and was picked up by radio and television, the letters, faxes and phone calls began to hit Ray's desk. Most of the so-called Christian callers condemned him for getting involved in the issue, saying (again) he should not step into the area of politics. Others accused Ray of siding with the ANC/Communist alliance or of aligning himself with the New World Order. I fielded many of the phone calls on Ray's behalf, and found the majority of the callers smallminded bigots. But sadly, they all did it in the name of Christ!

The local '702' radio station called Ray to confirm that he was voting 'yes' and to refute the 'Mark of the

Beast' scare, which they claimed was still the subject of dozens of phone calls each day.

Besides issuing a public statement Ray also circulated a letter to all the IFCC churches, so that they would be able to read the full text of his statement on the two matters and help them in guiding their congregations.

However, it was not only the man in the pew who got hot under the collar because of Ray's courage to state his convictions. A few church leaders took exception as well, among them Dr Izak Burger, head of the Apostolic Faith Mission, the oldest and largest Pentecostal denomination in South Africa.

The referendum issue became the focal point of a meeting of the newly-formed Pentecostal charismatic Fellowship of Southern Africa (PCFSA). A General Council meeting, held four days before the referendum date, resulted in a head-long clash between Black and White members as well as White on White.

Dr Burger sparked the controversial debate when he referred to one of Ray's press statements which appeared in an Afrikaans morning newspaper and which gave the impression that he was calling upon all Pentecostals and charismatics to vote 'yes'. Ray calmly, but firmly, stated that he took exception to the fact that his right to make a public statement was being questioned, and pointed out that he had not been speaking on behalf of the PCFSA.

It was clear that some of the PCFSA delegates, notably those representing the older, classical Pentecostal denominations, were not keen for any further statement to be made on the referendum issue.

Ray, as chairman, had gone into the meeting hoping that it would be possible to get a positive statement on the referendum issue. In fact, he had a draft statement in his pocket which called for a 'yes' vote. As the debate bounced around Ray got increasingly agitated. He turned to me at one stage and hurriedly whispered into my ear, wondering whether it was worthwhile to continue with the meeting. As secretary of the PCFSA I was taking minutes, and agreed that we might be faced with a crisis.

However, a final shoot-out was avoided when it was agreed that a statement had to be issued and a draft press release was speedily drawn up. The draft statement condemned any return to apartheid or any form of racism—which was the platform of the Right-Wing groups—but did not go so far as to call for an unequivocal 'yes'. As such, it did not make headline news.

On the positive side, however, the PCFSA had been preserved, because if there had been a showdown on the 'yes' issue the organisation would have been irreparably damaged.

In fairness, it must be said that Pentecostal denominational leaders who attended the meeting indicated that they would personally be voting 'yes'. Their problem, unfortunately, was that they were not prepared to give a public declaration and lead to their followers. Their plea to the meeting had been to be sensitive to the historical background of their churches, which had operated segregated congregations and had many churches in conservative, rural areas.

To Blacks that argument made no impact and drew no sympathy. They retorted that it was time for White Pentecostal Christians to be sensitive to the needs of their Black brothers and sisters.

In the end Christian grace had prevailed and the conservatively-minded White Pentecostals, once again, had been placated. Some emotions had been ruffled and the debate had brought forth some straight-talking which left the denominational Pentecostals in little doubt that they needed to do some hard self-examination and do something about the bigotry and racism which exist within some of their churches.

After the dust had settled from the meeting, all attention and energy were focused on the outcome of the referendum. Ray had called for a national day of prayer for the Sunday before the ballot, and a barrage of prayers bombarded heaven on March 15.

The intensity of the referendum issue was broken for a brief couple of hours when the South African cricketers beat India to reach the semi-finals of the World Cup! Ray was so delighted that he announced the result at the close of the Sunday morning service.

On the day before the referendum Ray was invited to be one of several special guests to sit on the platform of a 'Yes Rally' which was held at the Johannesburg City Hall. The speakers for the meeting were the Minister of Foreign Affairs, Mr Pik Botha, and the leader of the Democratic Party, Mr Zach de Beer. Ray, accompanied by Gordon Calmeyer and myself, went to the rally which was attended by over 1,000 people, who sacrificed their lunch hour to be at the meeting.

The purpose was to get as many celebrity guests at the meeting as possible who had come out publicly to vote 'yes'. Sports stars, retired politicians, key business executives, including the retired mining magnate Mr Harry Oppenheimer, entertainment personalities and religious leaders, turned out in force.

By trying to ensure that Ray got a prominent seat on the platform I manoeuvred Ray so that he would be in the forefront of the celebrity group when the signal came to walk down a passage and through a door which led directly onto the platform. When the signal came to the group I dutifully hustled Ray to the front, and with Gordon Calmeyer we ended up as the leading group which stepped out first onto the stage. As we did so loud applause and clapping broke out behind us. Ray, taken aback and slightly embarrassed, had not been aware that the audience was already seated in the hall, and he hurriedly sought out a chair and sat down.

Ray ended up sitting close to two rabbis and Bishop Peter Storey of the Methodist Church. The evening television news carried film of the rally, and Ray was easily identifiable on the front row, causing some consternation, again, to some confused Christians who could not understand the referendum as anything else but a moral issue.

Before entering the City Hall Ray had been stopped on the steps by a reporter for a comment, and one of the questions asked was what 'yes' percentage he anticipated. Without hesitation Ray said 70 per cent, which seemed to take the reporter aback. Most newspaper predictions and even the comments from some cabinet ministers, seemed to indicate that 60 per cent would be the most to be hoped for, and more likely to end up with a 55 per cent majority.

March 17 arrived, and nearly three million White South African voters went to the polls to make a decision which would have a profound impact on the future of thirty-two million Black people.

Ray voted in the mid-morning at a school hall nearby the church, and reports streamed in all day of a massive turn-out of voters. It was a day of waiting, because the counting of votes did not start until the following morning. Besides the Sunday prayers Ray had called for referendum day to be a day of prayer and fasting.

The day of the Big Count was a Wednesday, which coincided with Rhema's weekly Advisory Board meeting. During the morning Ray, in between a few official matters, stayed glued to the TV set, waiting and watching for the results. The Board meeting, which started at 1.00 pm, will probably rank as the quickest ever held, as Ray made it plain that he wanted to get back to the TV and the results.

He need not have been anxious, because the 'yes' voters carried the day with a decisive 68 per cent majority, only two percentage points less than Ray had predicted.

The euphoria in Ray's office was heightened by President de Klerk's speech in Cape Town when he publicly declared that once and for all the majority of White people in South Africa had rejected apartheid and all of its racist implications.

The Right-Wing leaders, mortally wounded by the result, offered some lame excuses, but it was obvious to all level-minded people that South Africa was indeed heading for new and exciting horizons.

South Africa, an outcast from the international community for so long, was at last being welcomed back.

Many people, some obscure, some famous, have worked tirelessly—and continue to do so—for this new day. Some have been in the struggle all their lives. Others, like Ray, are newcomers to the battle for righteousness and justice.

Each contributes something of value and importance to restoring dignity to a nation that almost died of shame.

APPENDIX A

The Rustenburg Confession

The following is the text of the sermon and confession of Ray McCauley made at the Rustenburg Conference of Churches held in South Africa in November 1990.

I would like to quote from the book of John on the subject of unity.

> My prayer is not for them alone. I pray also for those who will believe in me through their message, that all may be one, Father, just as you are in me and I am in you. May they also be in us so that the world may believe that you have sent me. I have given them the glory that you gave me, that they may be one as we are one: I in them and you in me. May they be brought to complete unity to let the world know that you sent me and loved them even as you have loved me.
>
> (John 17:20–23)

I would like to discuss what I mean about unity and the practical ways I believe the Lord is leading us, by His Spirit, into this unity.

Firstly, I do not mean a unity of doctrine, but a unity of witness in the faith. But, before some of you shut yourself off from me or formulate an impression of me without ever having met me, just give some thought to what I have to say, as what I say comes from the heart. I think it is important for us to realise, and at the Conference I have come to this realisation, that we often have more things in common than not.

I would like to discuss a unity, not of doctrine but of witness, and how that unity was manifested at the Conference has been nothing short of a miracle for our nation.

Ephesians 4:13 says: '. . . until we all reach unity in the faith and in the knowledge of the Son of God and become mature, attaining to the whole measure of the fullness of Christ.' And I believe we are beginning to see a maturity come forth in the body of Christ in a wonderful way. I believe we have two common factors with which we can all identify. We are all serving the same Lord, *and* we are fighting the same devil.

Secondly, I talk about a unity in the church that will produce unity in our country. I believe that the church, as a whole, should lead the way in our country, and that the politicians should follow the church and not the church follow the politicians. I believe there is a prophetic voice which is growing stronger and stronger on the basis of unity.

Many of you might say that we have been leading the way. Yes, but I am saying, 'Just relax and wait for us, we are catching up, and we want to be right in the forefront with you.'

John 17:22 says, 'I have given them the glory that you gave me, that they may be one as we are one.' And we must be one before we can expect South Africa to be one. There is so much in many of our churches—racism, bitterness and hatred—and yet we want to tell the people out there what they have to do and what we expect of them. But if we do not get our act together, and if we do not walk in unity, harmony, love, forgiveness, repentance and justice, then can we possibly call on anybody else to do so? I think we first have to get our own house in order, before we can expect anybody else to do so.

Apartheid has worked so well in our own churches,

separating us from our brothers and sisters. What I have missed most in fellowship is the opportunity to learn and to grow. We have separated ourselves so much that we have often lived in different worlds. Thank God that wall has now come down in my own life.

Unity will produce a strength in the church in South Africa that has never been seen before. I believe that the church is going to become the glorious church, a place of profound influence and strength, and is going to be increasingly influential (not that it has not already been) in the next ten years or so.

> Then they said, 'Come, let us build ourselves a city, with a tower that reaches to the heavens, so that we may make a name for ourselves and not be scattered over the face of the whole earth.' But the Lord came down to see the city and the tower that the men were building. The Lord said, 'If as one people speaking the same language they have begun to do this, then nothing they plan to do will be impossible for them.'
>
> (Genesis 11:4-6)

And I honestly believe with all my heart that what has begun to take place in this country, and at this Conference, is going to shake this nation into realisation. I honestly believe that what is currently taking place through the Holy Spirit, is going to have a profound effect.

Archbishop Desmond Tutu said that God is a God of the miraculous. What I believe, is that He can take us into a dimension of unity never before seen in the history of South Africa. I want to believe with all my heart that, when it looks so impossible, when it looks so difficult, when it looks that it cannot be done, the God of the impossible is still in control, and that we will go from one level of unity to another.

How can we obtain this unity? I believe that it has to begin in our hearts. It is very difficult to speak to people or to minister to anybody who says: 'I dare you to bless me. Just try!'

A few years ago, the Lord began to deal with me in my heart on a number of things I had done wrong: on the issue of ministering to the poor, the social side, reaching out and helping people who need help; on the issue of being involved in a lot of the problems where we had previously just sat back and done nothing. I pray that God will continue to do that work in my heart, so that I may reach the place of 'Thy will be done' in my heart and life.

But God has to do the work in our hearts. God has to speak to our hearts, and we have to be open to receive.

Secondly, we must put aside our own kingdoms. Often we say we have, but I watch people and it is so comfortable to be in your little domain, in a position where everything is perfect.

Please do not put me in a box. Someone once asked me: 'Aren't you from the First Prospertarian Church?' Please do not put me in a box. Speak to me if you want to help me, if you want to give me an opportunity to change. The best definition I have ever heard from a pioneer is that constant change is here to stay. So often we want to categorise people, and we warn against one another. And yet, after talking to them for just a little while, I find out that they love Jesus more than I do.

I believe that tne time has come for denominations, organisations, or whatever we may call them, to get dimmer, and for the name of Jesus to get brighter until all we can see is Jesus.

> Jesus knew their thoughts and said to them, 'Every kingdom divided against itself will be ruined, and every city or household divided against itself will not stand.'
>
> (Matthew 12:25)

That is one of the strategies of the devil. If he can divide us, he can conquer us.

Matthew 6:33 says: 'But seek first his kingdom and his righteousness, and all these things will be given to you as well.'

Thirdly, for the unity to increase after the Conference, we need to make a decision for the love of God to be poured out in our hearts. I believe the time has come for the love of God to take prominence in our actions, our reactions, in the way we conduct our lives.

During a recent holiday, I was sitting on a beach on the South Coast with my seven-year-old son, Joshua. We were having a good time, and the beach was full. A group of young teenagers came walking down the beach, and I could see the white people getting tense. These were young black teenagers. They sat on the edge of the beach, and no one said anything to them. Two white kids were tossing a ball to each other. One black kid went over to them and asked if he could play with them. They refused. I saw this young man go back and sit down, and I saw the despair and confusion and hurt in his face.

I had just bought a brand new football for my son and I said: 'Joshua, will you go and give them your ball?' He said: 'Daddy, it would be a pleasure.' He picked up that ball and walked over to them and said: 'I would like you to have this ball and play with it. Not only play with it, but have it.' I then saw hope come back in this young man's eyes, and he came up to me and he said 'Thank you, sir,' and within ten minutes, all the white kids were playing soccer with the black kids! That whole situation had been defused by one seven-year-old boy, showing love when others refused.

Repentance is essential, but so is forgiveness! Let the love of God be shared in our hearts. I want to share with you a testimony to the love of God in a person's life. Perhaps you heard of the couple who were lost and found themselves in a suburb of Soweto.

They were approached by thugs and, in the ensuing altercation, shots were fired. The woman was shot, and the bullet bounced off a bone and killed her husband. The couple were from New Zealand, and their kids and family are members of our church. This woman, Phyllis Harrison, is a committed Christian, and from the hour that incident took place, she would not allow it to be politicised or become anything of a racial issue.

She said it was pure thuggery and at the funeral she came to me and said: 'Pastor, I have forgiven them.' Her strength, and the love that she projected in a time of tragedy, were an inspiration to me. And if she can do that, how much more can we as the church turn around and say: 'My brother, I forgive you because the love of God is in my heart.'

> If I (can) speak in tongues of men and (even) of angels, but have not love (that reasoning, intentional, spiritual devotion such as is inspired by God's love for and in us), I am only a noisy gong or a clanging cymbal.
> (1 Corinthians 13:1, The Amplified Bible)

And unfortunately there are many 'cruisamatics', as we call them (you may call them charismatics), that are like that.

> And if I have prophetic powers—that is, the gift of interpreting the divine will and purpose; and understand all the secret truths and mysteries and possess all knowledge, and if I have (sufficient) faith so that I can remove mountains, but have not love (God's love in me) I am nothing—a useless nobody. Even if I dole out all that I have to the poor in (providing) food, and if I surrender my body to be burned (or in order that I may have glory), but have not love (God's love in me), I gain nothing. Love endures long and is patient.
> (1 Corinthians 13:2–4, The Amplified Bible)

Be patient with me.

> Love is kind: love never is envious nor boils over with jealousy; is not boastful or vainglorious, does not display itself haughtily. It is not conceited—arrogant and inflated with pride; it is not rude (unmannerly), and does not act unbecomingly. Love (God's love in us) does not insist on its own rights or its own way, for it is not self-seeking; it is not touchy or fretful or resentful; it takes no account of the evil done it—pays no attention to a suffered wrong. It does not rejoice at injustice and unrighteousness, but rejoices when right and truth prevail.
> (1 Corinthians 13:4–6, The Amplified Bible)

The Lord began to do a work in some of the brethren at the Conference. Please understand that this comes by what we believe the Lord is saying in the whole of the Holy Spirit at this Conference.

In order to face the future and to offer hope to the nation, I think it is crucial that we deal with the past in regard to the charismatic churches, and I would like to read a formal confession, made on behalf of Rhema, the IFCC, the Christian Ministries Network, and Christian Fellowship International.

Despite our short history, we recognise our guilt in that, for some of us, our opposition to apartheid did not go far enough, nor was it effectively expressed, while others of us adopted a so-called neutral stance which resulted in complicity in the system. Our statements and conviction were often not adequately put into practical action. As a result, we were often silent when our sisters and brothers were suffering persecution.

We confess that our silence in these areas was in fact a sin. And that our failure to act decisively against all forms of apartheid made us party to an inhuman political ideology.

We therefore confess our failure and repent of our sin and declare our complete rejection of all forms of racism and the evil, unjust system of apartheid. Please forgive us.

Further, as part of the family of God, we declare our resolve to play an active and positive role in ensuring that all people receive an equal opportunity to take part in all forms of political, economic and social life in the post-apartheid South Africa.

Please forgive us.

APPENDIX B
The IFCC Statement

The following policy statement regarding relevant socio-political issues was drawn up by the International Fellowship of Christian Churches (IFCC), of which Ray McCauley is a leader, and was made public in September 1991.

In releasing the document Ray McCauley, on behalf of the leadership of the IFCC, said the policy statement had become necessary so as to give a clear biblical lead to the nation, concerning specific issues which were part of the debate for the future of South Africa.

The policy statement touched on basic issues of apartheid, violence, the economy, capitalism, socialism, extreme political groups, politics and the pulpit, and employer-employee relationships.

The following is the full text of the policy statement.

Apartheid

IFCC rejects any form of separation or discrimination based on the colour of one's skin. The word of God clearly indicates that there is no discrimination in the kingdom of God.

Violence

Violence in any form must be condemned, particularly if this is used to bring about political, economic and social change.

Violence may give the impression of getting results, but these are only temporary. Violent actions cannot achieve racial justice. Violence is not only immoral, it is also impracticable. Dr Martin Luther King, Junior, said violence is 'immoral because it seeks to annihilate the opponent rather than seek his understanding . . . it thrives on hatred rather than love . . . it destroys communities and makes brotherhood impossible . . . it leaves society in a monologue rather than dialogue. Violence ends up by defeating itself.'

Current South African economy

The South African economy is a mixture of capitalistic and socialistic systems. It is, by and large, an interventionist economy. It is largely or was largely discriminatory and heavily biased against Black economic progress.

IFCC expresses its disapproval of a discriminatory economy against Black people.

The IFCC calls for an economy that is biblically based and not controlled by central government.

Free-enterprise economy

An unselfish capitalist or free-enterprise economy is biblical, but South Africa today is not expressing a true capitalist economy. The present form of capitalism in South Africa is blamed, in some quarters, for the increasing poverty and unemployment etc. This is not correct because the unemployment, poverty and declining economy are because of a mixed economy.

Capitalism is attacked on the ground that it exploits poor people and poorer nations, that poverty is the result of exploitation and oppression by someone who profits from the poverty of others.

IFCC believes that a biblically-based free enterprise system allows individuals the freedom to buy and sell, save and invest, choose their preferred form of employment and develop their own skills of their own free will. A capitalistic system that hoards and refuses to voluntarily share its wealth is unbiblical and is rejected by the IFCC.

Socialism

Socialism, enforced by an all-powerful central Government, is an economic system that replaces the free-market spirit and deprives the labourer of a fair reward for his effort. A socialistic economy lowers productivity and denies people the incentive to achieve and succeed, which are basic God-given attributes.

IFCC rejects a socialistic economic system as unscriptural, believing it will lead to further poverty and unemployment in South Africa.

Extreme right and left organisations

Extreme coercion by organisations not based on the second-greatest commandment—love thy neighbour as thyself—is unscriptural and therefore disapproved of and condemned by IFCC.

Politics in the pulpit

IFCC discourages pastors from being involved in party politics as this could split and introduce strife in congregations.

Pastors should encourage their people to judge politicians on Christian morals and ethics, and to challenge them on issues that are contrary to the word of God. Pastors should not encourage their members to join any particular party.

IFCC will distance itself from pastors who are members of political organisations.

Employer-employee relations

IFCC calls on all pastors, as employers, not to show any form of discrimination in their ministries in the way of salaries, wages and promotions.